Newspapers and Computers
An Industry in Transition

Newspapers and Computers
An Industry in Transition

By
Peter Desbarats

Research contributions to
Newspapers and Computers—
An Industry in Transition:

Morrison W. Hewitt
Michael Tyler
Jean-Paul Lafrance
Ian Brown

Robert Collison
Tom Paskal
Institute for Research
on Public Policy
Charles Dalfen

Volume 8
Research Publications

Royal Commission on Newspapers

Tom Kent
Chairman

Laurent Picard
Commissioner

Borden Spears
Commissioner

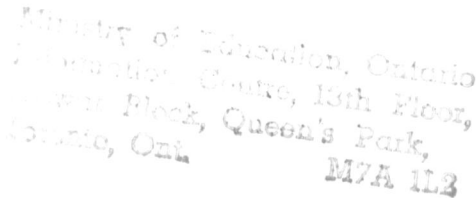

© Minister of Supply and Services Canada 1981

Available in Canada through
authorized bookstore agents
and other bookstores
or by mail from
Canadian Government Publishing Centre
Supply and Services Canada
Ottawa, Canada, K1A 0S9

Catalogue No. Z 1-1980/1-41-8E Canada: $5.95
ISBN 0-660-11063-6 Other Countries: $7.15

Price subject to change without notice

Contents

Research publications VII
Introduction IX
1 Newspapers and computers 1
2 Newspapers in the information society 7
3 Videotex: the new medium 15
4 Communications: the Canadian tradition 21
5 Videotex: theory and practice 25
6 Telidon 45
7 Videotex: Canadian field trials 51
8 Canadian newspapers and the information society 61
9 The future of videotex 67
10 Protecting the individual 71
11 Protecting the nation 77
12 Freedom of the electronic press 83
13 Concentration of ownership 95
14 Information, knowledge, newspapers, and new ideas 101
15 Postscript: the new literacy 107

Appendices
I Research contributors 110
II Selected bibliography 111
Index

Research publications of the Royal Commission on Newspapers

Volume 1 *Newspapers and their Readers,* by the Communications Research Center, with an introductory chapter by Leonard Kubas.

Volume 2 *The Journalists,* by Robert Fulford, Lysiane Gagnon, Florian Sauvageau, George Bain, Walter Stewart, Gérald LeBlanc, Dominique Clift, Tom Sloan, Pierre Ivan Laroche, and Jean Cloutier.

Volume 3 *Newspapers and the Law,* by Walter Tarnopolsky, Colin Wright, Gérald-A. Beaudoin, and Edith Cody-Rice.

Volume 4 *The Newspaper as a Business,* by Eugene Hallman, P.F. Oliphant and R.C. White, and Communications Research Center.

Volume 5 *Labor Relations in the Newspaper Industry,* by Gérard Hébert, and C.R.P. Fraser and Sharon Angel, Allan Patterson, John Kervin, Donald Swartz and Eugene Swimmer, Pierre-Paul Proulx, and James Thwaites.

Volume 6 *Canadian News Services,* by Carman Cumming, Mario Cardinal, and Peter Johansen.

Volume 7 *The Newspaper and Public Affairs,* by Frederick J. Fletcher, with contributions from David V.J. Bell, André Blais, Jean Crête, and William O. Gilsdorf.

Volume 8 *Newspapers and Computers: An Industry in Transition,* by Peter Desbarats, with the research assistance of Morrison W. Hewitt, Michael Tyler, Jean-Paul Lafrance, Ian Brown, Robert Collison, Tom Paskal, the Institute for Research on Public Policy, and Charles Dalfen.

Note: The numbering of the volumes reflects the order in which their subject matter is taken up in the Commission's Report.

Introduction

This study originated in the belief of Tom Kent, chairman of the Royal Commission on Newspapers, that the Commission's research in new information technology should be undertaken by a journalist rather than a specialist in computers or communications. I welcomed the opportunity. My main conclusion, for the Commission, my fellow journalists, and others involved with newspapers, is that we all have a great deal to learn — and little time in which to do it.

At the Commission, Tim Creery, the director of research, contributed his own lively curiosity about new technology, as well as the example of his own industry, and his enthusiasm for the Commission's work. Chief counsel for the Commission, Donald S. Affleck, Q.C., helped guide me through the regulatory maze of the communications world. Nicholas Gwyn, secretary of the Commission, used his familiarity with the Ottawa bureaucracy to simplify my own task.

I relied heavily on many others. Morrison W. Hewitt, senior partner with Woods Gordon, Toronto, provided me with the first comprehensive survey of computerization of daily and weekly newspapers in Canada, accompanied by his own insights. Charles Dalfen, former vice-chairman of the Canadian Radio-television and Telecommunications Commission, now with an Ottawa law firm, assembled an impressive array of documentation for his study of regulatory aspects of the new technology. Ian Brown and Robert Collison, freelance Toronto journalists, did a beautiful job of investigative reporting in their study of Canadian newspapers' involvement in videotex. Tom Paskal, formerly with the Montréal *Star*, provided an essential log of videotex trials in Canada. At the Université du Québec, Jean-Paul Lafrance and his colleagues gave me the benefit of their own research into Québec media and new technologies. All these studies have been deposited with the Public Archives. (A complete list is found in this volume as Appendix I.)

From the start, the writings and advice of Douglas Parkhill, assistant deputy minister of the Department of Communications, the real "father" of Telidon and a remarkable public servant, were invaluable. Michael Tyler, of Communications Studies and Planning International, in the process of shifting the base of his activities from London to New York, contributed his own awareness of developments in Europe and Canada, as well as his growing familiarity with a more complex scene in the United States.

Sherrill Owen, director of the Commission's Information Centre, helped to discipline my own somewhat freewheeling research procedures, and Louise Plummer painstakingly transformed the results of all this from manuscript pages covered with hieroglyphic corrections to clean printouts from the word processor. The meticulous indexing work in this volume was done by Bibiane Poirier. All these activities would not have come together so efficiently and productively without the dedicated guidance of Dick MacDonald, co-ordinating editor of research publications.

As was the case with other Commission researchers, I was encouraged to draw my own conclusions, in addition to providing factual information. Consequently, these do not necessarily coincide with the conclusions of other researchers or with those of the Commission itself on the basis of all the evidence gathered in the course of its public hearings and supplementary inquiries.

Finally, to the University of Western Ontario, my thanks for their patience in allowing me to complete my work for the Commission before taking up my duties as Dean of Western's School of Journalism.

Peter Desbarats
London, Ontario

1
Newspapers and computers

Canadian newspapers have undergone a technological revolution in the past decade. The introduction of computers, barely under way when the Special Senate Committee under the chairmanship of Senator Keith Davey published its Report on Mass Media in 1970, has changed the appearance and function of the editorial departments of most of our newspapers.

Reporters no longer sit at battered Remingtons, whisky on their breath, cigarettes dangling from their lips, intoxicated with their own significance. Copy boys no longer attend them to carry sheets of the latest news from typewriter rollers to screaming editors across the room. It's all done quietly and electronically now. In air-conditioned newsrooms, the journalists discreetly play legato on the keys of computer terminals. They look like airline reservation clerks, perhaps a little less harried. Softly tapping their terminals, editors summon stories from the memories of computers, process them, and assign them for typesetting.

Little more than 10 years ago, even on the largest newspapers, typesetting was an arcane craft performed in hot, noisy composing rooms under the baleful eyes of compositors who barely tolerated the interference of editors with the columns of type in their intricate metal pages. In a nest of reading lamps, somewhere in the depths of the composing room, proofreaders, as learned, as hermetic, and as poor as monks in a medieval scriptorium, cackled over the follies of this insane world. The composing room has vanished; not even a few scraps of paper remain behind. In glass-walled chambers chill and silent as tombs, computers now set "cold type" on film, infinitely faster and more accurately than did the linotype operators who used to cast type from hot metal. Nearby, survivors of the old composing rooms tamely paste up positive images of the filmed type into newspaper pages ready to be photographed and transformed into printing plates. And the days even of this menial occupation are numbered.

This revolutionary change has come perhaps not as dramatically as forecast in the late 1960s, but with dazzling speed compared with the previous 60 years. There had been little innovation in the production of newspapers since the introduction of the linotype at the end of the 19th century. The arrival of computers in newspapers in the 1960s heralded changes even more important than the mechanical improvements of the previous century. This event is now often described as part of an information revolution as significant as the one created by the invention of moveable type in the 15th century and the spread of the printed word as a means of mass communication.

In the early years of this revolution, computers have helped some newspapers to survive in competition with electronic media. The struggle will become more difficult. If computers continue to make electronic information systems more versatile and viable, they may emerge from their glassy cages to destroy newspapers — at least as we have known them for generations.

The 1970s have been called "the decade of internal reorganization" for newspapers, largely because of developments in Canada, the United States, and Japan. Whatever the future holds for newspapers, it will become evident first in those countries. On a smaller scale and with some delay, Canada has followed changes in the United States, where computer systems used by Canadian newspapers have originated.

Canadian newspapers' first computers, in the late 1960s, were simply added to existing "hot metal" typesetting systems. They were able to hyphenate words and create symmetrical columns of type. Relieved of these tasks, linotype operators could keypunch text into paper tape about twice as fast as their former speed on a linotype machine. By feeding the paper tape into the computer for hyphenation and justification, and linking the computer to a linotype machine equipped for automatic operation, it was possible to double or triple the production of the machine. This initial use of computers still required operators to key the text into paper tape and supervisors to monitor the typesetting equipment. Net savings were modest for the relatively few newspapers, probably less than a dozen across Canada, that installed this equipment. It had little effect outside the composing rooms of newspapers; editorial and most other departments continued to operate more or less as they had for the previous half-century.

Widespread use of computers awaited the development and adoption of photocomposition units able to produce "cold type" on film to replace the metal type of the linotype machines. This equipment was developed in the 1960s and widely used in the 1970s. Eventually, the two technologies merged with the design of computerized photocomposition units, making it possible for reporters and editors, in effect, to set type on their computer terminals, with most composing room operations being performed by the computer.

Rapid adoption of computer hardware by newspapers isn't common to all developed countries. Craft unions in many European countries have been more successful than the International Typographical Union in North America in delaying the introduction of computers. In 1980, only 41 European newspapers had computer terminals in their newsrooms.[1] In some of these newspapers, members of craft unions, not journalists, had the exclusive right to man the keyboards of terminals.

Terminals began to appear in Canadian newsrooms in the early 1970s.[2] There are now more than 1,200 video display terminals (VDTs) used for inputting and editing text in Canadian newspapers. Editors on the copy desks of virtually all Canadian newspapers with daily circulations of more than 40,000 are using VDTs for editing; on all but a few of these newspapers, reporters are typing their stories on VDTs.

There are still a few newspapers of this size where reporters type stories on sheets of paper that are "read" by a scanner attached to the computer, but this appears to be transitional and outmoded technology.

The use of computers isn't limited to large metropolitan dailies. Almost half Canada's small newspapers, with daily circulations of less than 10,000 copies, use VDTs for writing and editing. Only 25 per cent of medium-sized newspapers, with circulations from 10,000 to 40,000, have computers in their newsrooms, mainly because most of the computer systems on the market in the past decade were inappropriate for papers of this size. These newspapers are expected to catch up with the others in the next five years as the cost of computer equipment continues to decline.

Reports from various wire services can be fed directly into newspaper computers. Not only do virtually all large Canadian newspapers receive wire copy in this way but more than one-third of the small newspapers have this capability. More than half the large newspapers also have on-line terminals in news bureaus outside their main offices and can equip their reporters in the field with portable terminals.

From the outset of these changes, in the late 1960s, computers were designed for many other newspaper activities. The "newspaper of the future", originally expected to arrive by 1980, was seen extending the use of computers to display and classified advertising, press control, mailroom stacking, and business systems. It was forecast that VDTs with large screens capable of displaying a full page would be used to make up news and advertising pages. Computers then would be able to produce film images of complete pages to be transformed into printing plates by photocomposition. That would end the paste-up of cold type, the last vestige of composing-room craft to be made obsolete by the computer.

Some of these developments have been slower than expected. Virtually all large newspapers in Canada now use computers for classified advertising but only four report that they are capable of "pagination" — the making up of all or part of a page of ads on the terminal screen. Less than half of the smaller newspapers use VDTs to key ads directly into the computer rather than first typing or writing them on paper. Fewer than half the largest newspapers have the ability to display large advertisements on their terminal screens so that these ads can be composed by the computer rather than pasted up by hand. The introduction of computers into the printing and mailroom handling of newspapers also has been relatively slow. The "newspaper of the future", in its entirety, will take at least twice as long to arrive as originally expected. Instead of 1980, the target year is now located somewhere in the late 1980s or early 1990s.

The reasons for progressing slowly were both technical and human. It was more difficult than expected to develop computer systems that newspapers found profitable. Early uses of computers in news and composing departments saved time and money; savings were less dramatic in other departments. There were personnel difficulties. Suppliers of computer systems and equipment for newspapers in the 1970s often experienced financial problems and, in some cases, went out of business.

The process is taking longer than expected, but the trend is unmistakable. A report for the U.K. Royal Commission on the Press in 1975 stated that "the revolution has now gone so far, and built up such a momentum, that there is now no alternative path".[3] Canadian newspapers have accepted this in practice. Although it will be five to 10 years before complete on-line news text editing photocomposition systems are installed in virtually all Canadian newspapers, our larger newspapers will move into more advanced systems during these years.

Five large newspapers now have the ability to display and edit part of a news page on a terminal screen. Of the rest, in this group, all except one expect to have news pagination within the next decade. Within the next five years, pagination of classified ads and the use of large-screen VDTs for display ads are expected to be in use in most large dailies.

A member of the Gannett group in the United States, Westchester Rockland Newspapers in Harrison, N.Y., began creating full pages on newsroom terminals in January, 1981. Other American newspapers are experimenting with pagination, as are newspapers in Belgium, Switzerland, France, West Germany, and Finland. In the early 1970s, the Toronto *Star* was part of an abortive IBM attempt to create a pagination system.

Full pagination necessarily will precede laser platemaking under the direct guidance of the computer, eliminating photographic or chemical processing in the production of the printing plate. When all this has been achieved, perhaps in the late 1980s or early 1990s according to the current expectations of large Canadian newspapers, it will be possible for the journalist to place a report directly and instantly on a printing plate. The computer will be able to alter the plate as quickly as it now can change words or images on a television screen.

The same technological development that has helped some daily newspapers to survive in competition with electronic media has strengthened the weekly press in competition with dailies and other media. Although statistics on the weekly press are less comprehensive than for daily newspapers, it is clear that weeklies have grown substantially in numbers, circulation, and prosperity in the past 10 years. Weekly community newspapers have shown an increase in editorial and economic vigor that contrasts with the performance of the daily press during the same period. Computers have contributed to this although they have not been the primary factor. More important was the initial switch from letterpress production using hot metal to cold-type offset printing. In fact, weeklies made this change more rapidly than dailies. Almost one-third of the weeklies surveyed for the Royal Commission had converted to cold type by 1970; five years later, more than eight out of 10 weeklies had switched to cold type. At that time, only six out of 10 Canadian dailies had discontinued hot metal operations.

During the past decade, weekly newspapers have strengthened their editorial coverage and improved the marketing of their advertising space through national and provincial associations. In total, these developments and the switch to offset printing probably have been more important than the introduction of computers.

About 40 per cent of the weeklies surveyed for the Commission have computer equipment with all the basic characteristics of the largest systems used by daily newspapers. One out of five weeklies plans to upgrade this equipment within the next two years, and half the weeklies anticipate doing this within three to five years, an indication of the flourishing state of this sector of the newspaper industry.

Computers and offset printing clearly have made it easier to start and operate weekly newspapers. Although a few weeklies have become dailies during this period, there is no sign that the prosperous computerized weekly press is a seed-bed of new daily newspapers. There may even be a contrary indication. Computer-based typesetting systems have encouraged the consolidation of production facilities for weeklies and a tendency toward group ownership. About one-third of the weeklies surveyed for the Commission are published through joint facilities producing up to 10 or more weekly newspapers. In some cases, these facilities are owned by daily newspapers taking advantage of the growth in community newspapers and attempting to protect themselves from it.

Reporters and editors on Canadian newspapers have adapted quickly and relatively smoothly to working with computers, despite some fears about the hazards of low-level radiation from VDTs. A number of early studies have shown that editing on computer terminals rather than on paper is more accurate although it also may be more time-consuming. A detailed study of one U.S. newspaper in the 1970s[4] showed that the use of computers reduced typographical, spelling, punctuation and hyphenation errors, contrary to early fears that the elimination of proofreading would increase the number of published mistakes. Once editors and reporters become accustomed to the new system, they tend to prefer it.

In theory, computers could increase the journalists' control over the final product. Only electronic circuits and machinery, eventually, will stand between journalists and the printed page. Journalists will be in a position to control the entire apparatus of production. Technical control, however, will be meaningless unless the authority of the editor or journalist matches this new capability. Otherwise, the new technology will make journalists, even more than they now are, appendages of the machine.

Computers already have enhanced the ability of accountants to oversee and perhaps to control every aspect of newspaper operations, even from remote head offices of newspaper groups. The role of advertising departments may expand in future if computerized subscription lists, containing data on each reader, make the newspaper and its advertising part of much larger promotion and marketing operations.

The full effect of computers on the internal structure of newspapers awaits the completion of newspapers' "internal revolution" in the next decade, but the major economic benefits of computers for the competitive position of newspapers, as carriers of both news and advertising, already have been felt. Proprietors and managers of almost all Canadian newspapers believe that the use of computers has increased efficiency, reduced costs, and improved the quality of the editorial product. It is unlikely that later generations of computer equipment will produce the same dramatic reductions in cost as did the elimination of such functions as linotype operation, proofreading, and the manual composition of pages in metal.

An essential aspect of the newspaper of the future, envisaged in the late 1960s, was the use of computers to automate newspaper "morgues" or libraries. It was anticipated that newspaper content would be culled daily for items of lasting value that would be stored in a computerized library system. This "database" was expected to be not only an electronic "morgue" for the newspaper itself, but a basic provider of information in a future society where many people, so it was believed, would be able to access newspaper archives directly on their own computer terminals.

One newspaper, the Toronto *Globe and Mail*, launched its library into the computer age in 1979 and today markets its database through its subsidiary, Info Globe. Several other large Canadian newspapers have begun the costly process of recording their archives electronically but in this branch of editorial activity, further changes will be made slowly. There appears to be little interest even among other large newspapers in extending the use of computers to their libraries in the foreseeable future — a significant intention, or lack of it, for Canadian newspapers about to find themselves encountering new forms of competition in an emerging information society.

References

1. Nick Russell, "News according to the New Technology." *Content*, July-August, 1980. p. 13.
2. Morrison W. Hewitt (Woods Gordon), *Newspapers and Computers.* Research study for the Royal Commission on Newspapers, 1981. Public Archives.
3. Rex Winsbury, *New Technology and the Press.* Study for the Royal Commission on the Press. London: HMSO, 1975.
4. Starr D. Randall, "The Effects of Electronic Editing on Error Rate of Newspapers." *Journalism Quarterly*, Spring, 1979. p. 161-165.

2
Newspapers in the information society

Internal changes in newspapers are only one expression of a more fundamental technological revolution involving the introduction of computers and the creation of global systems of telecommunication.

First used during the Second World War, computers originally were massive and expensive. Their widespread adoption awaited the development of integrated circuits in the 1960s. Since then, computers have become constantly smaller and cheaper. Simpler computer languages, closer to ordinary speech, have contributed to their usefulness.

As mankind discovered how to store vast numbers of information "units" in the memories of computers, the concurrent development of telecommunications networks using such systems as microwave links on earth, undersea cables, and satellites in space created the ability to transmit the computers' seemingly infinite store of information almost instantly between any points on the globe.

In combination, these technologies represent the most potent development of man's intellectual ability since the invention of printing. Some scholars believe that the economic impact of the marriage of computers and telecommunications will be akin to the changes that followed the introduction of machinery at the beginning of the Industrial Revolution. They foresee mankind, led by the developed industrial countries, progressing from an industrial society to an "information society" where the production and transmission of information becomes the primary wealth-generating activity.

This process is further advanced than many of us realize. Although we have become used to the convenience and frustrations of business accounting and billing by computer, the scale and extent of computer operations is largely hidden from us. Computing has remained anonymous and mysterious, despite the fact that it affects and supervises intimate aspects of our everyday life, and that our livelihood increasingly depends on computers as does mankind's ability to carry forward co-operative ventures in such activities as trade, agriculture, engineering, defence, and the exploration of space. Canadian businesses already are so dependent on computers that back-up service to cope with the breakdown of commercial computer systems is an essential part of the industry.

Journalists find themselves among a multiplying number of people who earn their living at the terminals of computers. An international survey toward the end of the 1970s estimated that five to 10 million visual display terminals (VDTs) were then in use.[1]

Continued development of computers and further advances in the transmission of information appear to be inevitable, barring a global catastrophe or some form of massive social rejection of this technology. In the view of many theorists, the impact of these technical advances on human activity will be forceful enough to create a new kind of society.

This emerging information society is compared, in the United States, with its predecessors, the agricultural society and the industrial society that developed in the 19th and 20th centuries. About halfway through this century, another fundamental shift in occupations began as more and more people became involved in the handling and processing of information rather than the production of food or manufactured goods.

The United States is said to be in the midst of a transition from an industrial to an information society; some studies already describe it as the world's first information society. There is still uncertainty about the current extent and pace of the transformation but little about the direction of the trend.

It is assumed by most students of the information society that its human components will live and work in ways novel to us. It will no longer be necessary for people to go to work, it is said; work will go to people. The computer terminals that everyone will possess will be used not only for instruction, personal communication, and business transactions but for creating the basic product of the information society. Information itself will be the origin of wealth. Status in the new society will be intellectual rather than economic.

Intellectuals have had fun in recent years speculating wishfully about a society of intellectuals where they finally would come into their own. More realistically, they have been aware that basic assumptions about the information society remain untested. Information, for instance, may not be a commodity that can be readily bought and sold. When commodities are traded now in the marketplace, sellers relinquish them physically to purchasers. This doesn't happen with information. It remains in the possession of the seller after it has been transmitted to a buyer. In fact, its value may be enhanced after it has been widely disseminated.

All the current theories about the information society expose the absence of any accepted theory. As one of Canada's most perceptive participants in this emerging society has observed, "Our past economic experience has done little to prepare us for the task of identifying exactly how a society can generate real wealth by simply shuffling information around." Gordon B. Thompson, of Bell-Northern Research in Ottawa, also has suggested that "perhaps information economics is to conventional economics as Einstein's Theory of Relativity is to Newton's Theory of Gravitation." If this is true, no one has yet demonstrated it; and Thompson has warned, "To design an information system for public use without such a theoretical basis is like attempting modern physics without Einstein's contribution."[2]

Prepared or not, Canada is rushing into the new era in the wake of the United States. One of the leading theorists of the information society in the United States estimated more than five years ago that about half of the American work force already could be classified as information workers.[3] By this definition, the information sector of the Canadian economy was employing at that time from 40 to 45 per cent of our workers.

Uncertainty about the way in which information will behave economically is matched by doubts about human behavior in an information society.

One response to this has been utopian. The new technologies have inspired reams of hopeful imaginative literature. According to some theorists, they will make mankind less homogeneous. The new media will enhance individualism; every man will be both a user and supplier of information. Energy will be conserved because people will work at home, plugged into huge information networks which will be the most vital public utilities of the future. The design of these "mass information utilities", according to one writer, will be critical for society because it will be "no less than our design of the new individualism".[4] Out of these changes will emerge, in the most hopeful prospectuses, communities where private greed is no longer equated with public good. These unselfish societies of the future, in a world based on an information economy, will share knowledge with one another, trading in a commodity that increases in value as it is bought and sold. Because of this unique quality of information, according to an American communications expert, "the information game can be played on a global scale as an 'everybody wins' game rather than the 'winners and losers' game that is played with material resources."[5]

Not all the forecasts are as sanguine. Students of the new technology also have foreseen societies where individuals cannot possibly cope with the amounts of data stored in computers and circulating among them. In an effort to control what some have called an "information explosion", or to escape from what others have called an "information deluge", societies may decide to entrust affairs to small and dedicated "priesthoods of knowledge".[6]

Centralized control of information not only would tend to increase social and economic divisions in society, but could eventually paralyze it. Bureaucratic systems have an insatiable demand for information. Without the insight and imagination of gifted individuals working in a free society, accumulated data eventually would clog the information systems. Even in the early stages of development, the new information systems exhibit this characteristic; the technology seems to outstrip man's ability to provide it with meaningful content and purpose.

If individuals and societies are unable to cope with huge increases in our ability to record and transmit data, future-shocked consumers may try in the 1980s to curb runaway technology. Marshall McLuhan predicted this.[7] Or, they may accept the technology passively. People might become "electronic hermits" utterly dependent on computers to satisfy their needs and desires. Even man's image of himself and his society would be processed and perhaps manipulated by the computer.

Nightmare scenarios so far have had no effect on the rapid development of computers and telecommunications. In a world of dwindling natural resources, these technologies still appear to hold out the prospect of an increase in mankind's ability to employ these resources effectively. They continue to be regarded hopefully as a means to discover new sources of physical and intellectual energy.

Newspapers are on the breaking crest of this technological wave because their business is, in part, storage and transmission of information. These aspects of the newspaper industry, as we have seen, already have been changed almost beyond recognition in the past decade and they will continue to evolve within newspapers in predictable fashion in the near future.

In the meantime, aspects of the newspaper business other than production and marketing — the origination of information, the accumulation of knowledge, and the distillation of wisdom — have been little affected by the computer. Their development, in fact, may have been retarded. As the means of processing and distributing information have improved within newspapers, relatively little attention has been paid to the declining quality of the information. In this respect, the newspaper may be a microcosm of the emerging information society, a baleful harbinger of its dangers as well as an example of its efficiency.

As the capacity of computers grows and the transmission speed of communications increases, the role of newspapers will continue to be affected, although no one knows how quickly or how drastically. Forecasts in the past decade of the imminent death of newspapers already have proved to be premature. This has led to more recent predictions that newspapers, having survived so far, will adapt somehow to new competition and remain indefinitely, in much their present form, as important carriers of information and advertising. This seems unlikely in view of the accelerating development of new methods of transmitting both news and advertising in fresher and more usable condition.

The wisdom of the moment is that daily newspapers as they now exist — monopoly newspapers in most cases with computer experts to keep them abreast of technological change — will be able to maintain circulation and advertising revenue for at least the next five years, probably the next 10 years, possibly longer.

The recent durability of some newspapers during the gestation of the new electronic media, and early problems with the experimental hardware and use of these media, have created a new conservatism about media technology. Influenced by the relatively slow growth of new systems in the United Kingdom, the only country in the world to progress from experiments to commercial operation, many experts now are tempering their early enthusiasm. Rex Winsbury, a journalist active in the development of British systems and a leading authority on the new media, now believes that it will be "a very long time, if ever" before the new systems can compete with the low cost and convenience of newspapers.[8] The same viewpoint is now expressed by Roy Megarry, publisher of the *Globe and Mail* of Toronto and one of the pioneers of new information systems in Canada. Only a few years ago, as vice-president of corporate development for Torstar Corporation Limited, in charge of developing new information systems for the owners of the Toronto *Star*, Megarry predicted that printed communications of all kinds, including newspapers, would shrink in volume as the new systems came into being. He warned newspapers that "classified advertising, the backbone of the newpaper's revenue base, is one of the most immediately viable data bases for the new home information systems."[9]

As publisher of the *Globe*, and an attentive student of the British experience, Megarry has revised his early forecast and now believes that newspapers will survive indefinitely, perhaps by evolving new forms to adapt to competition.

Gerald Haslam, a former journalist active in the exploration of new systems for Southam, told the Royal Commission that it is now "impossible to bring forward evidence" of a threat to newspapers from these systems.[10] Martin Goodman, president of the Toronto *Star*, in collaboration with Southam the leading commercial developer of the so-called "electronic newspaper" in Canada, has predicted that the conventional newspaper "is still going to be cheaper per month than cable or any of the add-ons". Print will survive, said Goodman, because it is "portable and an enduring record . . . TV is passive and washes over you".[11]

Neither the early panic nor current complacency in some quarters of the newspaper world seem justified by the current state of development of new systems. The panic was created by the theoretical potential of the new systems. The difficulty of building the first demonstration models has given rise to a new conservatism about their prospects. More relevant is the pattern of development in recent years. The money invested in devising and testing new information systems in a growing number of countries in the past three or four years has increased in a rising curve. There is every indication, particularly in the United States, that this trend will accelerate. It is hard to believe that development at this pace by so many groups in so many locations ultimately will come to nothing.

An American communications scholar in 1980 said that North American newspapers would retain a technological lead over newer systems "for the next several years" but that electronic delivery of information will become less and less expensive as newspaper production and distribution costs continue to rise.[12] Economic factors already are persuading some newspapers to prepare for the day when they might become the main promoters of new forms of delivery and the main providers of news and advertising for the new systems. "We must admit we are not in the newspaper business," one American newspaper executive has said, "for, if that is what we think, we will go the way of the railroad. Newspapers are in the communications business."[13]

A leading U.S. newspaper publisher, John Cowles Jr., chairman of the board of the Minneapolis Star and Tribune Co., has forecast that the "electronic newspaper" will be available on television screens and from hard-copy printers in the home and office by the year 2000.[14] Other American publishers have been concerned enough about this development to take court action to prevent the largest telephone utility in the U.S. from experimenting with home videotex services. The publisher of the London *Free Press* in Ontario has taken the same stance in calling telephone companies in Canada "the greatest single threat to daily newpapers".[15] Publishers and reporters in the United Kingdom have warned the British government about adverse effects on newspapers and appealed unsuccessfully for a moratorium on the development of new electronic information services. In France, the director of one of the country's largest regional newspapers said in 1980 that a loss of 10 to 15 per cent of advertising revenue to new media would endanger the majority of France's provincial daily newspapers. Newspaper publishers in France, Germany, and other European countries have succeeded in slowing down the introduction of new media.

The difficult and crucial question for the newspaper industry today is the form, extent, and timing of competition from these new systems. A number of large North American newspapers several years ago paid $125,000 each to a Boston consultant to be told, in summary, that they had little to worry about until 1990 but that their future after that date was uncertain. Most of the current studies are equally vague and, as far as newspapers are concerned, just as ominous.

The most recent and comprehensive Canadian study, by Data Laboratories of Montréal for the Institute for Research on Public Policy, has concluded that daily newspaper advertising revenue will not be threatened significantly by competition from various forms of electronic media up to 1985. It warns that this short-term pattern could change "quickly and discontinuously" in the late 1980s.[16]

Competition for the time and attention of newspaper readers and the dollars of newspaper advertisers is emerging in a number of forms: the extension of cable television services to include pay-TV; the growth of television received direct from satellites; increasing numbers of home video players using disc or tape; the spread of small computers into homes; and the development of videotex systems by television, telephone, or cable networks to provide print information on request on home television screens. All these forms of competition are now growing rapidly. Together, they clearly have the potential to affect newspapers, starting in the second half of this decade. The effect on newspapers could become critical in the 1990s.

In a limited sense, the new systems already are affecting newspaper operations. There has been some diversion of time and money by newspapers and newspaper groups into the development of these competitive systems. In Canada, for instance, Southam has curtailed its newspaper operations as it has increased spending, in concert with the Toronto *Star*, on the development of home videotex systems that would convey both news and advertising.

More precise forecasting of the effects on newspapers of these developments is difficult if not impossible because the new medium that appears to threaten them is still embryonic. Its technology is virtually untested in practice, its uses remain uncertain, and its future is a matter of speculation. The technology is so new that knowledge of its capability and understanding of its uses are far from widespread. Even the vocabulary of the new medium is incomplete and confusing.

References

1. M.J.E. Cooley, "Some Social Effects of Computerization" in *Man/ Computer Communication*. Infotech International Ltd., 1979, Vol. 2, p. 59.
2. Gordon B. Thompson, "How to Sell Nothing and Get Rich or Wealth Generation in an Information Society". Paper prepared for the 1980 Conference of the International Institute of Communications. Ottawa, September 10, 1980.
3. M. Porat, "The Information Economy." Ph.D. dissertation, Institute for Communications Research, Stanford University, 1976.
4. Harold Sackman, "Computers and Social Options," in *Human Choice and Computers*. American Elsevier, 1976.
5. Edwin B. Parker, "Social Implications of Computer/Telecoms Systems." *Telecommunications Policy*, December, 1976. p. 3-20.
6. Fred Emery, "Social Futures in a Wired World." *Telecommunications Policy*, June, 1980. p. 147-150.
7. Marshall McLuhan, in *Maclean's*, January 7, 1980. pp. 32-33.

8. Interview with Rex Winsbury, London, February, 1981.
9. A. Roy Megarry, "The Information Society". An Address to the Science Council of Canada, Ottawa, February 9, 1978. p. 33.
10. Royal Commission on Newspapers, *Transcript of Proceedings*, p. 2340.
11. Christopher Bain, "What, More Time in Front of TV?", Ottawa *Journal*, March 11, 1980. p. 7.
12. John C. LeGates, "Changes in the Information Industries - Their Strategic Implications for Newspapers." Speech to the Board of Directors of the American Newspaper Publishers Association, September 11, 1980, p. 16-17.
13. Alex de Bakcsy in "The Information Utility: An Alternative to Newspapers?" *Production News*, November, 1979. p. 13.
14. "What the Year 2000 Holds for Newspapers." *Editor and Publisher*, June 14, 1975. p. 28.
15. Royal Commission on Newspapers, *Transcript of Proceedings*, Walter J. Blackburn, p. 1897.
16. Data Laboratories, *Analysis of the Impact of Electronic Systems on the Advertising Revenue of Daily Newspapers*. Unpublished report for the Institute for Research on Public Policy and the Royal Commission on Newspapers. Montréal, 1981. Public Archives.

3
Videotex: the new medium

As yet there is no universally accepted term for the essential synthesis of the new technology — the marriage of computers and telecommunications to create what has often been called a new medium.

In 1976, before Canada aspired to a unique and perhaps leading role in the development of this technology, Douglas Parkhill, assistant deputy minister in the Department of Communications in Ottawa, expressed unhappiness with one of the terms in use at that time — *computer communications*. Computing, as he wrote, was only one of an almost limitless number of possible applications of the new systems. Parkhill suggested that terms such as *tele-information systems* or *informatics* might be more descriptive.[1] In 1978, two French theorists, Simon Nora and Alain Minc, produced a report on "L'informatisation de la Société" which not only had a catalytic effect on French policy toward *informatisation* but nominated another neologism — *télématique* — to describe the new phenomenon. This has occasionally been employed in anglicized form as *telematics*. American writers have coined the more awkward term *compunications*. One of the recent studies on the Canadian information society prepared for the Department of Communications suggested that *informediation* — an earlier Canadian coinage — should be replaced by *telecomputerization* to refer to "the societal penetration of telecommunications and computerization, together and individually".[2] In 1980, John Howkins, an editor at the International Institute of Communications in the United Kingdom, suggested that the French term *télématique* and its English version were proving to be the most popular to describe "the convergence of the telecommunications sector, the computer sector and broadcasting . . . into one massive industry".[3]

There is at least a commonly accepted term for the display of print on the television screen — *videotex*. This is the generic term most often used to describe print on the television screen when the television set is equipped to function as a computer terminal.

Used alone, the term usually describes information transmitted to the screen by telephone line or coaxial cable. Most of the videotex systems now being tested in Canada use ordinary telephone lines to bring print to television sets in homes or offices. Like telephone networks, these interactive videotex systems are two-way. Using typewriter-size keyboards with letters and numbers, or smaller keypads with only numbers and a few other symbols, videotex users can call up "pages" or "frames" or screenfuls of information stored in computers linked to the telephone network. They also can put information into the computers and use the system to send messages to other users.

Cable TV systems, if eventually they acquire the switching capacity that telephone networks now have, can be linked to computers and used as videotex networks.

Each system has its limitations at present. Telephone lines can carry only a limited number of information "bits", enough for the quick display of print on television screens but insufficient for photographic images. The coaxial cables of cable TV systems can carry more than enough "bits" for "picture videotex", with images and words, but it will be expensive to make these systems interactive and to give them the switching capacity, or its equivalent, that telephone networks possess.

There is a hybrid version of videotex that uses telephone lines to request information from computers and coaxial cables to transmit the information to users.

Conventional television channels also can be used to send videotex. The impulses or "bits" of information for the print display are transmitted in the "vertical blanking interval" of an ordinary television signal — the relatively small number of "lines" in the multi-lined signal that to now have been unused for picture or sound transmission. This "broadcast videotex" has come to be called *teletext*. The pages or frames of print are transmitted in a rapid cycle, over and over again. Television viewers with sets equipped to receive teletext can select and freeze pages from this cycle by pushing numbered buttons on small keypads.

Teletext is not interactive, and the number of pages is severely limited, for technical reasons, compared with the almost infinite number that can be stored in a videotex computer. The complete cycle of pages cannot take longer to broadcast than the time an ordinary user will wait for one of the numbered pages that he or she has requested. This effectively limits most teletext systems to a few hundred pages. Given that limitation, teletext is a much simpler and cheaper system than videotex by telephone line or coaxial cable for both users and producers. Canada's first trial of broadcast videotex was launched by TV Ontario in January, 1980. With the introduction of an experimental service by the Canadian Broadcasting Corporation, Canada is expected to join in 1982 the growing number of countries broadcasting teletext on national television networks.

Teletext can vastly expand its number of pages if a full television channel is used for teletext alone and if users' sets have additional equipment for storing and selecting pages.

Various countries have adopted "brand names" for their videotex and teletext services. The first operational videotex service in the world was called *Prestel* when it was announced by the British Post Office in 1978, after nearly a decade of development. The British also pioneered the use of teletext with licensed services on all their television networks in 1974. The British Broadcasting Corporation's system is called *Ceefax*; the Independent Broadcasting Authority has *Oracle*. The method used to display text and diagrams on the screen is called "alpha-mosaic" because it is a combination of letters and graphics created mosaic-fashion by assembling small units of color on the screen. Because of British expertise in this type of system, alpha-mosaic videotex is often referred to as Prestel-type.

When other European countries have adapted Prestel, they have given it their own "brand names". The West German Bundespost, for example, calls its experimental videotex service *Bildschirmtext*. In the Netherlands, it is *Viditel*; in Sweden, *Televerket*; in Finland, *Telset*; and so forth. All these are Prestel-type systems.

An American adaptation of Prestel, currently being tested in Florida by the Knight-Ridder newspaper group and American Telephone and Telegraph (AT&T), is called *Viewtron*.

Because of its complex written language, with at least 3,500 different characters, Japan has developed videotex with more sophisticated graphic displays than Prestel. Despite these improvements, its *Captain* videotex system displays less information per frame than European or North American systems and requires a much longer time, more than 10 seconds on average, to transmit a full frame to home screens using ordinary telephone lines.

In 1977, France developed its own alpha-mosaic system, *Antiope*, claiming that it produced better graphics than Prestel. Antiope also has been adapted for trials in the United States. The Canadian contribution to this glossary is *Telidon*, invented by researchers in the federal Department of Communications in 1978 and proclaimed internationally within months as videotex of the second generation. Telidon is an alpha-geometric system that displays, in addition to the usual text, graphics that are more refined than those of either Prestel or Antiope. Because geometric shapes can be created on the screen by Telidon more rapidly than by Prestel's square-by-square mosaic method, creation of videotex pages is simpler, but Telidon equipment so far has been more costly than the equipment needed to create and receive Prestel.

Telidon is, like Antiope, the name of a specific videotex and teletext technology, not the name of an experimental or operational system such as Prestel. In Canada, for instance, videotex in Ontario and Québec will be called Vista, the "brand name" selected by Bell Canada for its Telidon-type videotex system. As Telidon-type videotex or teletext systems are developed in other countries, they will have their own names.

Videotex and teletext systems, in summary, contain elements common to other computer and communications systems but in distinctive combination. Five essential elements were suggested in 1979 by the Department of Communications:

1. A remote source of information.
2. A telecommunications connection from the user to this source by radio wave, coaxial cable, copper wire, or optical fibre.
3. An information display that will often use a modified TV set with decoding capability.
4. A selection function on the part of the user, causing information to appear which is part of a larger selection offered by information providers.
5. A service designed for the mass market rather than a few specialist users.[4]

Most of the early writings on videotex have been produced by specialists involved in designing or evaluating experimental systems. Their purpose has been to explain videotex and to promote interest in it. Many of the academics writing about videotex have themselves been part of one of the earliest and, to date, the only profitable new videotex industry: the writing of books and articles, the production of academic papers, and the organizing of seminars and conferences on videotex. Most of the popular journalism about videotex has taken its enthusiastic and uncritical tone from these partisan activities. Typical of the current journalism on videotex is this description by a British science writer:

> Think of a system incorporating the computing, publishing, newspaper, broadcasting and library, telephone and postal services of the country, together with a large slice of teaching, of operations, and of many professional activities. All those... subsumed in one system will outstrip in magnitude and importance any industry or collective activity in which human beings have been previously engaged.[5]

More recently, with videotex systems operating in Britain and trial systems starting in many other countries, difficulties and deficiencies have become apparent. These have cast doubt on some of the early assumptions about the popularity of videotex. The industry, if it can be called that at this time, is still in the initial stages of discovering, in the words of a British communications expert, whether "electronic publishing for the specialist", which has existed for some time in such services as the electronic Information Bank of the New York *Times* or Info Globe of the *Globe and Mail* in Toronto, can develop into "a cheap, easily understood 'Model T' version of electronic publishing suitable for a much wider market among unsophisticated users".[6]

Technical limitations of current videotex systems, glossed over by most of the early writers, now have to be faced. Many of them are obvious to anyone who sees a working system for the first time: print on the television screen still is much harder to read than on the printed page; graphics on most systems look as if they were constructed from a child's Lego set; searching for information through successive frames of print on a television screen is a time-consuming and often frustrating experience; and relatively little information can be displayed on each frame or page.

Many operational problems remain to be overcome. In a typical home with one telephone line and one television set, normal use of the telephone and television is impossible while both systems are being used for videotex. The cost of home videotex equipment has remained high enough in Britain to discourage the development of a mass market. Serving a mass market will require heavy investment in equipment by telephone or cable TV companies.

Many of the early writers about videotex cited the growth of radio and television as precedents for the videotex industry. It already has become apparent that videotex, while it may not be a new medium in a technical sense but simply a new combination of existing technologies, is novel in its use by a mass audience. The radio and television audience is passive, waiting to be entertained and, occasionally, informed. Videotex requires the active participation of its audience. Videotex does not have listeners or viewers; it has users. Although it can be used for entertainment, videotex is more work than play.

No one yet knows whether people will want or need videotex. Certainly they will not pay money for it and devote time to it merely because the technology is ingenious. All the early tests have demonstrated that the novelty of videotex wears off quickly unless systems are useful. Although people will use videotex to play electronic games and to call up their horoscopes from computers, entertainment is not what videotex provides most effectively and efficiently. Its popularity will depend on the value to consumers of the services that it can provide.

Even at this stage, the services are bewildering to contemplate. At first, videotex was regarded mainly as a provider of information on demand. The data could be anything from the day's news, weather, and sports results to an electronic encyclopedia. In actual use, the ability of videotex to provide services such as shopping, airline bookings, and banking seems to be more important than the information function. In some of the latest videotex systems, the kind of news and information that journalists provide is no longer one of the primary services. Users, in future, may want videotex mainly for such practical tasks as paying their gas or hydro accounts, monitoring the security of their homes, or "teleshopping" for a wide variety of goods and services, and perhaps only incidentally for news.

Scenarios for the development of videotex, although more complex today than they were a few years ago, are nonetheless impressive. It is little more than 10 years since laboratory work started on Prestel. Telidon was devised less than three years ago. As promoters of videotex often recall, it required several decades for television to progress from the laboratory to the mass market. Because it uses many existing technologies, videotex has been able to develop more rapidly than television in the initial stage.

If it is technically a novel combination of existing technologies, videotex can be regarded as a new medium in terms of its potential impact on human existence. Perhaps it will be more important in the long run than radio or television.

In some respects, radio and television have had negative effects on human behavior. They often have entranced children, not stimulated them. Family conversation has been impoverished. Social life in the community has suffered, although in recent years there has been a conscious attempt to discover again the pleasures and uses of small communities of people defining and exploring their own interests, consciously breaking away from the mass audience that television and radio provide for the benefit of entertainers, journalists, and advertisers. Videotex systems will require the active participation of users. They will only be as effective as the users make them. The popularity of advertising or any other form of information on videotex, for instance, will be measured not in estimated numbers of viewers but in exact numbers of users. Videotex has the ability to break down the mass audience into small groups of users with common requirements or interests. It may reduce personal contact between people but it also might vastly increase our range of acquaintances. It is even conceivable that videotex might recreate an era when society prized the ability to write letters that were witty, elegant, and expressive. Videotex could have far greater effect on our social, political, economic, and intellectual lives than either radio or television. If this potential is realized, newspapers will be among the first of our institutions to feel the effects.

The alteration or disappearance of our conventional newspapers in competition with videotex would be only one symptom of fundamental changes in our national life. Videotex could have far more radical effects on our domestic political life and international relations than radio and television have had. If videotex systems are to develop extensively, they will do so within regulatory structures already in place in all developed countries. As they develop, they will alter not only these structures, in the first instance, but the character of all political and economic activity. Conceivably, the pace and quality of national development could be strongly influenced.

Because of the historical importance of communications in Canada, and because of our special reliance on modern communications for economic prosperity and cultural vitality, in few other countries would these effects be as rapid or as potent as they would be here.

References

1. Douglas Parkhill, "Who's Afraid of Computer Communications?" *In Search*. Autumn, 1976. p. 10.
2. Peter S. Sindell, *Public Policy and the Canadian Information Society*. Gamma, Université de Montréal/McGill, 1979. p. 4.
3. John Howkins, "The Information Societies". *In Search*, 7(2), Spring, 1980. p. 10.
4. John C. Madden, *Videotex in Canada*. Ottawa: Department of Communications, 1979. p. 3.
5. Nigel Calder, quoted by Val Sears in "The Robots Are Here." *The Toronto Star*, March 10, 1979. p. A18.
6. Michael Tyler, "Videotex, Prestel and Teletext." *Telecommunications Policy*, March, 1979. p. 37.

4
Communications: the Canadian tradition

Canada is in a favored position to understand this new technology, develop it, exploit it, and benefit from it.

We have a solid foundation of theoretical studies and practical development of modern communications. The theoretical base was created by such men as the economist Harold Innis, who died in 1952, and Marshall McLuhan, the media philosopher, who died in 1980. McLuhan, strongly influenced by Innis, altered mankind's appreciation of the influence of mass media. Innis developed a unique theory of the relationship of communications to history. As McLuhan wrote, Innis "taught us how to use the bias of culture and communication as an instrument of research...by directing attention to the bias or distorting power of the dominant imagery and technology of any culture, he showed us how to understand cultures".[1]

Almost 30 years after his death, Innis' thoughts about newspapers and radio are still used widely to assess later technologies. Anthony Smith, the British writer whose comprehensive treatment of the "newspaper revolution of the 1980s" was published in 1980, drew heavily on Innis' research to show that "it is arguably more revealing to use communication systems than production techniques as the boundary marks of history".[2]

The writings of Innis range across the centuries to illustrate his belief that changes in the means of communication have preceded and played major roles in religious, political, and economic reforms in many societies. Innis suggested that "we can perhaps assume that the use of a medium of communication over a long period of time...will eventually create a civilization in which life and flexibility will become exceedingly difficult to maintain."[3] Under this condition, a new medium emerges, leading ultimately to the creation of a new type of society.

In his own time, Innis was disturbed by centralizing trends reinforced by modern media. "The large-scale mechanization of knowledge," he wrote in 1947, "is characterized by imperfect competition and the active creation of monopolies in language which prevent understanding and hasten appeals to force."[4]

Although McLuhan later disagreed with him on this, Innis believed that the popularity of radio favored centralization and bureaucracy. In his note book in 1945,

Innis mused that "improved communication smothers ideas and restricts concentration and development of major ideas". He jotted down the phrase "mechanization and sterility of knowledge" as if to note a cause-and-effect relationship.[5] After Innis' death, McLuhan's explanation of the medium of communications itself as a statement about society and a major influence in shaping it — "the medium is the message" — intrigued a mass audience. At the very least, it helped everyone to look more objectively at the media as media influence became more pervasive.

That Canada has produced important theoretical work on communications is hardly surprising. Communications in various forms have been vital to the survival of this thinly populated nation. Innis himself came to the study of modern communications from research into the fur trade and early Canadian transportation. That era had barely ended when Canada entered the age of telecommunications. Less than two years after Samuel Morse, an American, invented the electric telegraph in 1844, Canada established the first commercial telegraph service between Toronto and Niagara. Canada was one of the first countries to develop telephone and telegraph communications technology on a large scale and has consistently pioneered new applications. "Canada is probably the world's most 'wired' society," noted an American communications expert in 1979.[6] More than 96 per cent of Canadian households have a telephone. Television is available to virtually the entire population; more than 40 per cent of the TV viewing market subscribes to cable TV.

Canada put the first operational domestic communications satellite system in place two years ahead of U.S. competition. Canadians also were the first to transmit a videotex signal overseas using a prototype direct-broadcast satellite to link a transmitter in Canada with an earth terminal in Australia small enough to fit on the roof of an ordinary house.

With the most advanced set of broadband local radio and television networks in the world, efficient telephone systems incorporating some of the most sophisticated electronic switching systems, two packet switching networks for transmitting computer data, and considerable satellite channel capacity and expertise, Canada is as well equipped as any nation to provide communication services needed by the information society. In the Nora-Minc report to the French government in 1978, the Canadian communications system was cited enviously as a model.[7]

Technical progress has been accompanied by thoughtful attempts to develop communications policy at federal and provincial levels. Earlier inquiries into print and broadcast media have been complemented since the late 1960s by a number of studies of computers and telecommunications. In the opinion of one U.S. observer writing in 1979:

> Canadian public policy reflects a far greater awareness than exists in the U.S.A. of the power which is exerted by communications and information resources. Unlike the U.S. government, the government of Canada looks at communications and information resources in an integrated fashion, and has gone to great lengths to study their role.[8]

The Canadian government's involvement dates from 1969, when the Telecommission Study reviewed the whole field of telecommunications. The Canadian Computer Communications Task Force in 1972 published "Branching Out", a report largely concerned with assuring the development of computer communications services in Canada in competition with data processing and data communications services based in the United States. In 1973, the government in Ottawa issued a "green paper" on computer communications that echoed the task force's concern about the role of multinational corporations in computer communications and, in particular, the question of Canadian jurisdiction over Canadian business data processed and stored outside the country. Another task force in 1972 dealt with privacy and computers, again with special attention to the legal and economic difficulties that might be posed by activities of U.S.-based data processing companies. The most recent major report on the future of telecommunications in Canada, the Clyne Report, was issued in 1979. There also has been a steady flow of specialized studies commissioned by government, and by agencies outside government such as the Science Council of Canada.

The first reports on computer communications tended to deal with such relatively well-defined questions as privacy of computer records and communications, and protection for Canada's electronic and data processing industries. Later inquiries revealed a deeper concern that computer communications might erode the cultural as well as the economic integrity of Canada. The Clyne Committee, for instance, was charged in its title with studying "the implications of Telecommunications for Canadian Sovereignty."[9] In announcing this study, Jeanne Sauvé, then minister of communications, listed the dangers that fibre optic communication, interactive television, and computer technology posed for Canada. It was feared that they might "radically increase the amount of American television programming entering the country; further aggravate the balance of payments problems in electronic products; increase the difficulties being experienced by the Post Office, schools and universities, publishing industries, and the clients they are meant to serve; and compromise the country's capacity to control future fundamental economic, political, social and cultural directions".[10] A draft telecommunications law, submitted to Parliament in 1978 but never enacted, expressed the same concern that a Canadian telecommunications system should "safeguard, enrich, and strengthen the cultural, political, and social, and economic fabric of Canada".

Lofty statements of principle in Canada have not always produced either coherent policies or the most rational development of communications systems. The translation of principle into policy has been hindered, at the origin of this process, by confusion about responsibilities and competition among various federal government departments and agencies. Decisions of regulatory agencies are sometimes at odds with directions taken by Crown corporations. The search for effective policies also has been complicated by the federal-provincial relationship in the field of communications which has been described as "at best, an uneasy compromise".[11] Communications is a federal responsibility but provincial jurisdiction over education and culture gives provincial governments a clear interest in the content of communications systems. There has been a proliferation across Canada of ministries and state agencies dealing with communications and pursuing separate and often antagonistic policies.

Co-operation between public and private sectors in this field remains primitive. Industry blames government for lack of support while the government complains about Canadian industry's lack of initiative. Distrust and suspicion hamper efforts to exploit Canadian expertise in communications in competition with other developed nations.

None of these difficulties is hidden or ignored in Canada. There is a constant effort to examine ourselves critically and to confront problems characteristic of our political system and our state of economic and technological development. Because of internal problems and the stimulus of competition from the United States, Canadian society has been traditionally vigilant if not always effective in protecting its own interests.

In communications, as in transportation in an earlier era, theoretical work and practical experience have helped us to define the public interest, and to develop a system of state enterprise and private initiative to serve our purposes. The history of telegraphic, telephone, radio, and television systems in Canada exhibits this concern and achievement perhaps more clearly than does the record of any of our other national endeavors. This strong tradition has been evident in our first approach to videotex and the emerging problems of the information society.

The decision to develop videotex in Canada was seen from the start, in the words of Jeanne Sauvé when she was minister of communications, as an "opportunity to introduce a system designed and manufactured by Canadians, and developed according to Canadian social and cultural needs". "It may be our last opportunity," she said, "to innovate and refine a Canadian technology that will ensure a strong domestic electronics industry and contribute to the strengthening and enrichment of our cultural sovereignty."[12]

References

1. Marshall McLuhan, Introduction to *The Bias of Communication*, by Harold A. Innis. University of Toronto Press, 1977. p. xi.
2. Anthony Smith, *Goodbye Gutenberg*. Oxford University Press, 1980. p. 322.
3. Harold A. Innis, *The Bias of Communication*. University of Toronto Press, 1977. p. 34.
4. Ibid., p. 29.
5. *The Idea File of Harold Adams Innis*. William Christian, ed., University of Toronto Press, 1980. p. 7.
6. Oswald H. Ganley, "Communications and Information Resources in Canada." *Telecommunications Policy*, December, 1979. p. 268.
7. Philippe Lemoine, "What Happened to Life Patterns?" Reflections on the Canadian Experience with Computerization. Supporting Document No. 3 for *The Computerization of Society* by Simon Nora and Alain Minc. Massachusetts Institute of Technology, 1980.
8. Ganley, "Communications and Information Resources in Canada". p. 270.
9. *Telecommunications and Canada*. Report of the Consultative Committee on the Implications of Telecommunications for Canadian Sovereignty. Ottawa, 1979.
10. Quoted in Ganley, "Communications and Information Resources in Canada". p. 289.
11. Kimon Valaskakis, *The Information Society: The Issue and the Choices*. Gamma/Université de Montréal/McGill, 1979. p. 37.
12. Jeanne Sauvé, quoted in Science Council of Canada, *Communications and Computers: Information and Canadian Society*, Ottawa, 1978. p. 38.

5
Videotex: theory and practice

Most of the literature on videotex to date has been produced by experts with an interest in seeing the technology develop as fast as possible. Whether it will develop rapidly and whether it will benefit mankind isn't as self-evident as proponents of the new information technology often pretend. Only now are we beginning to receive reports of initial experiences in creating and operating videotex systems. These early results have demolished much of the fanciful thinking about the "wired society" that proliferated in the 1970s.

Creating systems that link large numbers of people to information-distributing computers and, through the computers, to one another, will be more time-consuming and expensive than anyone imagined a few years ago. It is equally apparent that initial difficulties so far have not discouraged attempts to create such systems. The amount of money being spent on videotex in a growing number of countries increases every year. It will be astonishing if nothing emerges from all this activity but it is still impossible to tell what will emerge, and when, from the welter of competing experiments. There is competition, at the moment, between systems of videotex, between the means of delivering videotex to users' screens, and between corporations and countries manoeuvering for position in a vast potential international market for the hardware, software, and human talent that videotex systems would require.

The United Kingdom is far ahead of other countries in operating both videotex and teletext systems.

Like many great inventions, *Viewdata*, as it originally was called in Britain, was devised incidentally by an ingenious individual who had set out to develop something quite different. In the late 1960s, Sam Fedida, a British research engineer, was given the task of designing a computer system to keep track of vacancies in European hotels. His discovery that salaries and overhead in the central computer bureau would represent 80 per cent of the cost of such a system encouraged him to design a self-service operation to enable the customers themselves to search for hotel vacancies stored in a computer. Fedida was working along these lines when he joined the British Post Office (BPO) in 1970 and came into contact there with other researchers experimenting with *Viewphone*, a system like *Picturephone* in the United States and equally unsuccessful.

As the British researchers began to understand that telephone users might not need or want to see one another, they tried using the screens of their experimental *Viewphones* to display printed information. It was a short step from that to the notion of using the telephone system to display information on home television screens. In July, 1974, Fedida and his team of researchers demonstrated a working model of a videotex system to officials at the Post Office.

The decision of the British Post Office to promote videotex was almost equally incidental. The main attraction of videotex at the outset was a promise to increase Post Office revenues, a promise it has yet to keep. With only 60 per cent of British homes equipped with telephones at the time, the BPO saw videotex as a way to encourage telephone installation and usage.

In 1975, telephone and broadcasting organizations made a key decision to use the same terminal display standards for the Post Office's videotex system and the teletext systems under development by the two television organizations. This meant that all television sets in Britain eventually could have the ability to receive both videotex and teletext.

In 1978, the British Post Office christened its videotex system *Prestel*. A preview service was offered to the public in London in March, 1979; by the end of 1979, BPO was offering a full public service from two computer centres in London and one in Birmingham. The system had about 2,000 users, including sets issued for test purposes and those used by companies providing information to the system. There were more than 130 of these "information providers" at this stage; together they had assembled 160,000 pages of information on a wide range of subjects. To access this information, users required a specially equipped television set linked to the telephone system and to a keypad that enabled them to transmit numbers and a limited number of other instructions to the computer.

Prestel to date has hardly fulfilled the most limited expectations. By the end of 1980, there were only 7,310 users, primarily in the business world; only 917 of these terminals were in homes. The number of information providers had not expanded appreciably.[1]

The most apparent reason for the slow growth of Prestel is its high cost in comparison with other information systems. A color television set fully equipped for videotex sells in the United Kingdom for about $2,500. For the majority of Britons who rent their television sets, acquiring videotex adds about $12 to their monthly fee. To use Prestel, they also have to pay telephone charges and whatever fees-per-page are charged by the information providers. According to one estimate, these would amount to about $9 per month for a residential user who connected to Prestel once a day for a session of about three minutes.[2]

The system also is expensive for information providers. The average annual cost per page or frame, including BPO charges, editing, overhead, and promotion, was estimated recently to be about $60. A large database of more than 10,000 pages would cost at least $600,000 a year to maintain on Prestel.[3] One of the largest IPs in London had concluded by 1981 that "the economics of storing large amounts of information on Prestel were simply not attractive compared to other ways of doing it".[4]

The slow growth of the Prestel system has discouraged hardware manufacturers and information providers. In turn, the Post Office has criticized the manufacturers for failing to lower costs of videotex equipment through mass production, and information providers for slowness in developing databases attractive to the public. None of the participants in this vicious circle has seen a return on their considerable investment.

Britain also has led the world in the development of teletext as a part of everyday broadcasting. Engineers at the British Broadcasting Corporation experimented with teletext in the late 1960s; regular service, called *Ceefax*, was announced in 1972. The Independent Broadcasting Authority, which oversees Britain's commercial channels, demonstrated its system, *Oracle*, in 1973. As in the case of Prestel, both Ceefax and Oracle have had limited appeal because of relatively high costs. It was reported in 1979, five years after both services were licensed, that the price of a teletext-equipped set was still US $400 to US $600 above that of a conventional set. Manufacturers complained that they were unable to sell large inventories of sets built to receive teletext.

Early in 1979, manufacturers estimated that about 5,000 teletext-equipped sets were in use. The industry predicted that there would be 250,000 sets in use by the end of 1979. Growth has been steady but below these predicted levels. By the end of 1980, an estimated 100,000 television sets in Britain were equipped to receive teletext, and the total was growing at a rate of 10,000 per month by the spring of 1981. For the first time since the service was licensed, it was beginnning to reach an audience large enough to interest advertisers.

The BBC's Ceefax carries no advertising. Ceefax on BBC-1 offers about 100 pages of information: news, sports, and financial news. Ceefax on BBC-2 provides about 200 pages of background information on news stories. In addition to information, Oracle broadcasts advertising pages.

Compared with videotex, teletext is easy to start and cheap to operate. In 1979, Ceefax was being run by a team of journalists working in the headquarters of BBC Television in London. Only one or two persons were required to provide the news updates; the rest of the 16-person staff wrote book reviews, recipes, and other material for pages that were changed continually from 7 a.m. until midnight every day. Salaries for the Ceefax team in 1979 amounted to about US $300,000 a year; a new computer then being installed for Ceefax by the BBC cost about US $250,000. As one BBC executive noted at the time, this was about the cost of eight color cameras.[5] In comparison, the British Post Office allocated a budget of £23,000,000 in 1978 for Prestel, to purchase equipment for the test service, to establish computer-equipped service centres in more than a dozen major cities, and to finance the start of full service to the public. The estimated cost of building and operating a single Prestel service centre is estimated to be about US $1,000,000 a year.[6]

The most significant feature of Prestel, the one that has had a major impact on the development of Prestel itself and is now influencing videotex in every other country, is the absence of a strong and growing residential market. Originally, the home market was seen as the primary target. There already was "electronic publishing" for users in business, government, and various professions willing to pay for access to specialized databases. Videotex was to be a simpler and cheaper extension of this. It would bring the benefits of computer communications into millions of homes. Prestel was intended to become almost as much a part of everyday British existence as television, the telephone, the daily post, and the daily newspaper. In 1978, the British Post Office believed that there would be several million Prestel users in Britain by the end of 1983. It undertook an extensive advertising campaign in all media aimed in large part at the home market. By the end of 1980, with fewer than one out of every 10 Prestel sets in homes, BPO authorities abandoned the home market in practice, if not officially. Virtually all advertising and promotion is directed now toward potential business users.

Prestel did discover a receptive business market in some sectors. Among the most avid users of Prestel are travel agencies. Airlines, tour operators, and hotels list schedules, rates, and services in their Prestel databases, updating them continually. A start has been made on using Prestel to book space on aircraft and in hotels. When travel agencies discovered that their clerks saved time by using Prestel rather than the telephone, they soon became a major market for the service. Even some services originally designed for the home market were purchased by business users of Prestel. The most popular sections of the Prestel database, at least in the initial stage, were those devoted to astrology and computer games. So many of the requests for horoscopes came from businessmen that one provider of this service was thinking in 1981 of marketing a special business horoscope.

The failure of the home market to develop as expected created chaos among the more than 160 information providers already in the system. Some of them had invested heavily on the expectation of a large home market; none of the information providers had seen a return on their investment. In the words of one of them, early in 1981, "The domestic IPs are rushing around wondering what the hell has happened to them."[7]

Responsibility for this miscalculation is shared by many. Hindsight has shown that a system designed primarily by engineers, with insufficient advice from marketing experts, is headed for trouble as a commercial venture. "The domestic consumer in this country simply thought videotex was too expensive," according to one information provider. "There was a very high rejection rate."[8]

The real cost of preparing and storing information for videotex also proved to be higher than anticipated. In the early months, many large information providers charged rates that were lower than cost, writing off the loss as an investment in research and development. When this phase ended, costs began to escalate. "Once the real cost of storing information on Prestel was expressed in pounds and pence," said the same information provider, "and once you reckoned on the costs of getting information there in the first place, because of the amount of re-editing and general reorganization of data that has to take place, you were really facing quite substantial sums of money. And broadly speaking, you can only justify those expenditures by specialist information services for which you could charge a fairly high price."

Within the Prestel organization, social factors also are cited to explain the slow development of the domestic market and the shift of marketing strategy toward selected businesses. "Businesses are used to looking at screens to get information," explained a Prestel executive. "The private individual is not. He is used to looking at television as a purely passive entertainment medium."[9]

Prestel executives now expect that the domestic market will take "a couple of years to take off".[10]

Britain has, in summary, low-cost teletext systems that have succeeded in establishing a small domestic audience and a relatively high-cost videotex system used primarily by business.

Videotex promoters still believe that a reduction in costs will create a growing home market and that the current division — teletext for the home and videotex for the office — is temporary. Because information on teletext probably will always be limited and teletext systems will never be interactive, teletext is sometimes described as a transitional technology. This viewpoint is based partly on the untested assumption that teletext ultimately will be unable to meet the information requirements of the average consumer.

The decision to focus Prestel on the business market may change more than marketing strategies; it could alter the structure of the system. Information providers for business already have discovered that the costs of preparing and storing data in Prestel's central computers, owned and operated by the Post Office, are higher than expected. Some of them have concluded that the Prestel system is best used to communicate current information rather than to store large databases. Experience has shown that the large databases stored in Prestel were valuable only to a small number of people and were among the least used services, despite the high cost of storing this material in the central computers. As the cost of computers continues to decline, it seems to make more sense to think of storing large databases in third-party computers which can be accessed from time to time through Prestel. More recent videotex systems in Europe are being designed to have this "gateway" capability. It was expected to be available on Prestel late in 1981.

Although it may produce a more efficient system, the "gateway" technique also negates one of the basic principles of Prestel's original design. In creating Prestel, the British Post Office set out deliberately to build an "electronic highway" that, like a conventional highway, would be owned and maintained by the state and accessible to all. The role of the Post Office, as defined by itself, would be to "provide and manage an information distribution system, on a common carrier basis, and make it available to any organization wishing to display information, subject only to the law".[11] Information providers from the private sector would operate within this state-owned "marketplace of ideas" with competition based on price, service, and quality of information. To draw an analogy from print publishing, the state would own both the press and the distribution system but the pages would be open to all contributors or advertisers on an equal basis.

This accessibility, with the carrier of information completely divorced in theory from the information content in the system, is compromised when the state shares its right to store information with commercial competitors. The third-party databases then will decide what information and which information providers will be included in their indexes. The state system could become simply a "switchboard" connecting users and information providers to commercial databases which conceivably could be as powerful and as limited in number as print publishers are today. If this should occur, the accessibility that is such a prized feature of the original Prestel would disappear.

Prestel has given some British newspapers valuable experience in adapting to the new medium. Its database includes a news service, *Viewtel 202*, produced by The Birmingham Post and Mail Ltd., and advertising itself as the "first electronic newspaper" in the world. Other newspaper groups and publishers are involved in Prestel but the Birmingham *Post* is the only one providing a complete news service. Viewtel 202 was launched in January, 1980; several months later, it added paid advertising pages to the news pages that it offered without charge to Prestel users who keyed its call letters "202" to access its database.

Viewtel 202 looms large in the world of videotex as an innovative service but it occupies a small place in the parent company, the largest provincial daily newspaper publishing group in England. The Birmingham *Post* had few illusions about Prestel when it launched the new service. It had realized by then, as it stated in 1980, that "the whole cost structure of the Prestel project was actively against it becoming a low-cost media for information providers." The *Post* had decided that Prestel costs already were high enough to be "prohibitive for a rapid development of the medium in the mass market" and that the system "was in danger of becoming business oriented, with no cohesive development of the data in the system to enable an attractive package to be easily and cheaply available to the whole mass of potential users". This assessment "eased many of our concerns about Prestel's immediate impact on newspapers, but caused us major concern on the development of the medium as such".[12]

Viewtel 202 began modestly with a full-time staff of two—a journalist and an advertising salesman. Information was keyed into the system by compositors, members of the typographical union drawn from the parent newspaper. One year after its start, the editorial staff of Viewtel 202 had expanded only modestly, to an editor and two journalists. The service occupied 2,300 pages in the Prestel database. It listed 33 major advertisers, some with up to 100 pages in the Viewtel database, and more than twice that number of smaller advertisers with only a page or two. Viewtel's marketing manager, John Foxton, claimed in February, 1981, that the service would be not only covering its actual costs, including in-house services provided by the parent organization, but making a profit by the end of the year.[13]

Virtually all the news for Viewtel comes from the news services received by the Birmingham *Post* group. It is compressed and restructured for videotex. Rarely does a news story occupy more than one frame. If 100 people access the first frame of a multi-frame news story, experience has shown that only 90 will request a second frame and only 60 a third. Usage will be down to five or less if a fourth frame is offered. The most popular features are national news, sports, and horoscopes, in that order.

Advertisers who pay a sizeable premium — five times the top rate for an ordinary frame — can purchase an "adflash" that repeats a come-on message about their advertisement at the bottom of a news page and gives the page number of the advertisement. Even without this enticement, users of *Viewtel 202* spontaneously request many of the advertising pages.

The staff of *Viewtel 202* appear to believe that they already have achieved a virtual monopoly of the "electronic newspaper" business in the United Kingdom. They have learned how difficult it is to organize even a relatively simple news service on videotex. They believe that, once such a service is established, because of the abbreviated nature of the news as presented on videotex, a competitor would find it difficult to offer a distinctive product. These factors have persuaded the *Post* that its "national newspaper" on Prestel already is secure from competition, although regional "electronic newspapers" might have a role. The *Post* itself is exploring this possibility in its own area.

Viewtel also has learned that users of Prestel, with 250,000 pages of information in the system at the moment, soon become used to accessing a relatively small number of databases, perhaps four or five, and rarely venture into others. Once a news service or other information provider develops a clientele for its database, it becomes increasingly difficult for competitors to attract their attention. Advertisers search for databases with heavy page traffic, reinforcing their success in the same way as advertisers tend to help large newspapers to expand at the expense of their smaller competitors.

None of the legal problems inherent in videotex, particularly involving copyright and libel, seem to have disturbed the early years of Prestel. Perhaps this is partly due to the fact that information providers, having joined together in 1978 in an Association of Viewdata Information Providers, soon adopted a code for content, pricing, and advertising. This early attempt at self-regulation was tested in January, 1980, when the world's first electronic "Guide to Dirty Books" appeared in the Mills and Allen database, one of Prestel's largest. Although the *Daily Mail* and other newspapers devoted headlines to the "dial-a-pornographer" service of "Rupert Street-Walker", and the chairman of the Post Office was quoted as being "disappointed that an information provider has used Post Office facilities to display material that may be offensive", the infamous Guide was more parody than pornography and disappeared from Prestel before it caused any real trouble. During its short life, it served a useful and perhaps not unintended purpose by forcing the Post Office to repeat publicly its policy that "information providers who rent from us have complete commercial and editorial freedom within the constraints imposed by the law of the land to put in what they want".[14]

In practice, separation between carrier and content in Prestel is not always so clearly implemented. At times, shortage of computer capacity has forced the Post Office to choose between new information providers "on a commercial basis". Information providers have complained about being struck from the published directory of IPs issued by the Post Office because, in the BPO's view, the directory description did not match the information on the system or the IP's database was judged to be of poor quality.

Prestel doesn't try to conceal its control over the selection of information providers, despite official policy to the contrary and the difficulty of justifying it in law. As one Prestel official explained, Prestel is "exercising control over information providers. . .because there aren't sufficient pages at the moment. . .we're taking those who are going to create the most balanced, most attractive database".[15]

The British government has had little difficulty finding space in Prestel for its information. A 1980 statement by Sir John Barran of the United Kingdom Central Office of Information listed 20 government departments and agencies already represented in Prestel — everything from tax details from Inland Revenue and weather forecasts from the Meteorological Office to legal aid and advice schemes from the Lord Chancellor's Office. In his statement, Sir John raised the possibility that the state also could use interactive videotex to poll citizens about government policy or regulations, provided that privacy was respected. He also indicated that there is some official concern about the ability of information providers to regulate themselves.

"You cannot monitor several hundreds of thousands of frames, any one of which can be altered at a minute's notice," he stated, "... as the system grows, there will be more potential mavericks and then we may be in trouble."[16]

By being first in the field, by creating the first operational commercial videotex system in the world and, in the process, the largest on-line computer system ever designed, the British have learned more about the difficulties and potential of the new medium than anyone else. It has been an expensive experience and their investment is still speculative. At the moment, they seem determined to press this advantage by changing their system at home to meet the requirements that are now apparent, by selling Prestel International as a world videotex service, and by aggressively marketing Prestel technology and hardware, particularly in the United States.

The British experiment with Prestel is aimed at establishing a viable commercial videotex system, with state encouragement. France is the only country to attempt to become an information society by government decree. In France, according to current strategy, the new medium will arrive almost overnight, financed by massive state investment. The concept is Napoleonic in scope and ambition.

The principle of videotex development adopted by France is distinctive, at least in Europe. While the British struggle to develop progressively a mass consumer market for the new medium, France intends to create the market instantaneously by using the purchasing power of the state to equip millions of citizens with videotex sets. Voilà! The benefits of mass production are realized at once, the mass consumer market appears instantly, and France becomes another Japan as its huge electronics industry moves into world markets. In the process, French language and culture is rescued from the threat of assimilation by American computers that speak and think in English.

The great French leap into the electronic age is being watched by other countries with awe, apprehension, and some skepticism. Is it really possible, they wonder, to transform a nation that, until recently, was relatively primitive in terms of telecommunications into a world leader in *télématique* without a more conventional intermediate stage? Already it is apparent that the French concept is simple in design but complex to execute. It has encountered problems at the outset that arise from the essential nature of France — its history, its social structure, and the character of its people.

The philosophy of the French program was formulated in a report on "L'informatisation de la société" by two theorists, Simon Nora and Alain Minc. Published in 1978, their report not only outlined the features of the information society as forecast by theorists in other countries, particularly the United States and Japan, but galvanized French policymakers by its description of the latest version of "le défi américain". According to the Nora report, the multinational corporations based in the United States were in a position to dominate the European computer market and, ultimately, Europe's information industries. Nora and Minc warned that this posed a threat to French sovereignty, language, and culture.

In 1978, France was in the midst of an internal revolution in its domestic communications system. At the beginning of the decade, the telephone and telecommunications system had been described officially as "relatively under-developed and lagging far behind the networks of our foreign partners".[17] President Giscard D'Estaing determined in 1974 that improvement in this area would be a state priority. During the term of the sixth national plan, from 1971 to 1975, more than US $20 billion had been invested by the state in the telecommunications sector. In the following five years, this rate of investment doubled. The number of telephones grew by 18 per cent a year, one of the highest growth rates ever recorded by any country. The program created a cadre of 150,000 skilled workers and, as one American observer noted, "a vested budget item looking for the next thing to upgrade".[18]

Rapid expansion of the telephone system had meant constant updating and reprinting of telephone directories. The use of computers to maintain and typeset these lists led the French to explore the possibility of transmitting this information, including "yellow pages" advertising accompanied by graphics, directly from the computer to the subscriber. By 1979, the French had committed themselves in principle to the "electronic telephone directory" and had started to place initial orders for equipment.

The directory project is the symbolic Eiffel Tower of télématique. If it is successful, it will transform France's information sector. It will place its electronic industries in a position to dominate the European market and compete overseas with American and Japanese corporations. The plan is to give every telephone subscriber a small black-and-white videotex terminal instead of a printed directory. The French believe that the cost of providing an estimated 30,000,000 terminals over the next 10 to 12 years will be less than the cost of continuing to print telephone books and using operators to staff an inquiry service.

A preliminary trial was held in 1980 in St-Malo, the seaport used by Jacques Cartier in the 16th century as a base for his exploration of the New World. A full-scale trial was expected to start late in 1981 at Ille-et-Vilaine in the greater Rennes area of Britanny, involving all 250,000 telephone subscribers in the region within a few years.

Prototypes of the directory terminal have seven-inch screens and typewriter-style keyboards with numbers and letters. Although the first terminals will cost about US $250 each, this is expected to decrease to about US $100 within several years. Subscribers will be able to request telephone numbers or the addresses of other subscribers by typing information on their keyboards. There will be a small charge for this service. They also will be able to access the "yellow pages" of the electronic directory where businesses will display, on one or more frames, the goods, services, and prices that they offer. How often this commercial information will be updated remains to be decided.

Because these small terminals use the videotex system that is standard in France, they could be employed in future to access many other kinds of information. The system potentially is far more than an electronic telephone directory. If installed, it will give France the first national videotex system. France will become a prototype of the information society.

In tandem with the electronic directory, France is developing a conventional interactive videotex system called *Teletel*. The first trial, involving 2,500 sets, was expected to begin late in 1981. From the outset, Teletel will be a "gateway" system providing access to third-party computers, the French having decided that the original Prestel design was mistaken.

France also has a teletext service broadcasting to a limited audience. One of the distinctive features of French teletext is the use of entire television channels rather than the vertical blanking interval of conventional telecasts, as in Britain. Use of a full channel increases the number of pages carried by the service. There are 11 teletext "magazines" in operation on such subjects as stock exchange quotations, news, weather, traffic reports, and consumer information.

All French videotex and teletext services use the same standard — *Antiope* — a distinctive videotex technology for coding and display of information. Antiope is a sophisticated alphamosaic system, similar to Prestel but said to be more versatile in its ability to reproduce graphics.

Through a subsidiary company based in Washington, D.C., Antiope Videotex Systems Inc., the French have energetically promoted Antiope in the United States. The system has been tested by CBS and PBS stations and proposed to the Federal Communications Commission as the standard system for the United States. The French also have explored the use of Antiope in educational computer systems in the U.S., with Control Data Corporation, and have discussed joint marketing with Tymshare Inc., a U.S. computer service company. France and Canada signed a three-year agreement in 1979 for an exchange of information on Antiope and Telidon.

On the home front, early in 1981, the massive videotex campaign ran into political difficulties. French newspapers, alarmed by the scale of the proposed videotex systems and their advertising potential, slowly but surely organized a defensive strategy, using all the political leverage at their disposal. By the time of the presidential campaign in 1981, the press had succeeded in bringing the development of videotex to a virtual standstill, at least for the duration of the campaign.

Unlike newspapers in North America, the press in France has yet to experience a widespread internal revolution. There are no video display terminals in the newsrooms of Parisian dailies and few in the provinces. One of the basic obstacles to the introduction of computers, according to the journalists themselves, is the inability of many of them to type their own stories. They prefer either to write their reports in longhand or to dictate them to typists. Newspapers in France foresee a period of expensive internal technological change coinciding with a threat to their advertising revenues from videotex. The director-general of a large provincial daily, *Ouest-France*, accused the state telephone, telegraph, and postal monopoly in 1980 of using the electronic telephone directory to achieve its real purpose, the "development of a multitude of telematic services which will threaten the existence of the printed press and ultimately disrupt our national life".[19]

Within the state communications bureaucracy, officials unhesitatingly identify the press as their most formidable opponent.[20] The dispute is evolving quickly into a debate about the role of the press in a democratic society. French newspapers claim that this role is fundamental, and cannot be replaced by videotex. In response, the bureaucracy has launched studies which it suspects may show that the press overestimates its own influence on public opinion.

Pressure from newspapers created a political threat toward the end of 1980 to block the telecommunications budget in the National Assembly. The government responded by appointing a parliamentary commission to study the videotex trials, promising that it would not proceed with the electronic directory without consulting parliament. The newspapers have wrung several important concessions in principle from government: that only newspapers have the right to place classified ads on videotex, that enterprises can offer on videotex only services which they provide in the course of their normal business, and that videotex information providers cannot offer free services as an inducement to users. Proponents of videotex claim that the ultimate objective of the newspapers is to monopolize advertising on videotex to acquire new revenues to pay for the modernization of the printed press. They also forecast that the attempt will fail. Newspapers, it is claimed, will find it impossible to maintain a common front against videotex as more and more individual newspapers seek to exploit the new medium in their own interest.

Relatively little is known about the reaction of the French public to videotex. The technocrats have been curiously reticent about the preliminary trial in St-Malo. Apparently about 50 terminals were involved. According to one source in the computer hardware industry, telephone subscribers, most of them unfamiliar with keyboards of any description, had as much difficulty communicating with the computer as the computer had understanding them.[21]

The next few years will be crucial for France's innovative attempt to impose the information society by government fiat. On trial is the basic premise of the grand design, as defined by one of the men in charge of executing it: "Nobody is ready to buy a computer terminal now for the home, but if people have a terminal, they will use it."[22]

A struggle by newspapers for control of the new medium also has shaped the early development of videotex in West Germany.

Under the constitution of the Federal Republic, the printed press is a responsibility of the federal government, as is the telephone, telegraph, and postal service. Radio and TV stations are non-profit public corporations established and regulated by the Lander (state governments). From the outset, newspaper publishers in Germany have insisted that videotex is simply printed text in another form, that it is an extension of their current activity, and that it should not be regulated by government. Broadcasters have seen it as a development of their programming activity and have cited a 1961 Supreme Court decision which ruled that only companies set up under the public law, as opposed to private enterprise, could provide program material.

Despite this unresolved dispute, television stations are broadcasting an experimental teletext service with some pages allocated by regulation to individual newspapers. In 1981, the newspapers were occupying this space as a matter of principle, transmitting promotional material rather than inaugurating news and information services.[23] Newspapers insist on calling this service *Bildschirmzeitung*, a term for videotex that incorporates the German word for newspaper.

Bildschirmtext is the trial videotex service, based on Prestel technology, announced by the Bundespost in 1977 and launched in 1979 in Berlin, and in Dusseldorf the following year. There are several thousand users in each city. Like the French system, *Bildschirmtext* uses a host computer that functions as a gateway to third-party computers. Transaction services such as banking and shopping are an important aspect of these trials.

Most other western European nations have shown interest in videotex and have started trials of some type, initially following the British example and using Prestel technology.

Finland launched a commercial videotex system in 1980, *Telesat*, operated by a company formed by a national newspaper publisher, the largest privately-owned telephone company, and a computer terminal manufacturer. There is also a commercial videotex business service.

Sweden started a small trial in 1979, with newspapers and the Swedish Central News Agency participating along with other industries.

The Netherlands, despite regulatory confusion as to whether videotex is a broadcasting or telephone activity, is testing a public videotex service, *Viditel*, with 2,500 users as of April, 1981.

Switzerland purchased Prestel technology in 1979 for a small trial.

Belgium is testing two teletext systems, using Ceefax for the Flemish and Antiope for the French.

Other western European nations with trials in prospect are Austria, in collaboration with the German Bundespost; Denmark; Italy, with a system designed primarily for business use; Norway; and Spain.

Overseas, Australia has licensed experimental teletext transmissions since 1977. The federal government approved teletext broadcasting as part of the regular service of television networks in 1980. Teletext advertising was authorized at the same time. The British Ceefax system is used.

A videotex service based on Prestel has been announced by Telecom Australia, starting in late 1981.

Prestel is being used as the basic technology for a commercial videotex service in Hong Kong that started in 1980.

Japan has led the world, as a matter of policy, toward the information society. Its 1967 "Plan for the Information Society" was the beginning of a prolonged and concerted effort to give Japan a strong domestic electronics industry, protected at the outset from foreign competition, and aimed at capturing a large share of international markets.

As one observer has noted, the oil crisis in the 1970s and world shifts in the balance of economic and political power further persuaded the Japanese that the manufacture of cars, cameras, tape recorders, and other relatively sophisticated products would not provide them indefinitely with continued increases in their standard of living. The solution for Japan was "simple and blazingly unambiguous ... to make itself the number one computer power of the 1980s, designing, making and selling the stupendous range of computers and computer-based products which the world of a decade hence would crave".[24]

In addition to close co-operation between industry and government, long-range investment planning, and a disciplined labor force, Japan possessed a domestic market uniquely suited to test the apparatus of the information society. Western observers have noted in Japan the absence of the "peculiarly Western concept of man versus machine".[25] It is said that in Japan there is a "total lack of debate on the privacy or '1984' issues" that complicate planning for the information society in many other countries.[26] Not surprisingly, Japan has pioneered the development of videotex, teletext, and related systems. Its early field trials were attracting international attention when most European systems, apart from the British, were still in the laboratory.

Like Britain, France, and Canada, but for a distinctive reason — the complexity of the written Japanese language — Japan has created its own videotex system. *Captain*, an acronym for Character and Pattern Telephone Access Information Network, was developed during the years 1976 to 1978 when the Japanese conducted a complex interactive cable television experiment in Tama New Town near Tokyo. In 1978, Captain was selected as the videotex system for an extensive field trial in Tokyo that began at the end of 1979. By the fall of 1980, there were 700 residential users and 100 business users. The total number of users was expected to reach 1,500 in 1981. The database in the fall of 1980 consisted of 50,000 frames supplied by 180 information providers; the objective was a database of 100,000 frames with an average of 500 frames being updated every day. The information is divided into 16 categories. As of the summer of 1980, the most popular categories, judged by frequency of access, were: entertainment and hobbies (especially games and horoscopes) — 34 per cent; news and weather — 21 per cent; education and cultural — 14 per cent; sports — six per cent; and shopping — six per cent. These results parallel early experience in Western trials.

Japan's public broadcasting corporation (NHK) began a teletext trial in 1977 in the Tokyo and Osaka regions, using a small database of 30 to 40 frames.

In addition to videotex and teletext trials, Japan has an experimental optical fibre local network serving 150 residential users in Higashi-Ikoma near Osaka and Kyoto. The HI-OVIS system (Highly-Interactive Optical Visual Information System) launched in 1972 is "cabletext" rather than videotex, using full television channels to transmit print to home television screens. Because of the great transmission capacity of fibre optical cable, the system is able to provide 29 video channels to each user. The elaborate home terminals include a TV set, keyboard, small TV camera, microphone, and associated control and communications equipment. The Japanese intend to extend this system to five more cities eventually with about 2,000 users in each city for the duration of the trials.

The development of videotex in Japan has had to overcome a special problem. Japanese industry and culture may be custom-made for the information society but the Japanese language is not. Captain successfully handles the complex requirements of the Japanese language, with at least 3,500 characters and symbols, but not without paying a penalty. Because the amount of information required for the complex Captain image is larger than for a Prestel, Antiope, or Telidon frame, it takes longer to transmit. This peculiar handicap of Japanese videotex has been overcome, in the business sector, by abandoning written Japanese. *Nihon Keizai Shimbun*, Japan's leading business newspaper, now operates an on-line computer information system for business customers using the Roman alphabet but this solution is not useful for the mass market.

The language problem is expected to retard the development of videotex in Japan. One Western observer, after a thorough study of the Japanese systems, forecast in 1980 that there would be little development of substantial videotex markets or databases in the next five years and only modest development of teletext and cabletext. It was felt that this probably would be enough to keep Japan's electronics industry abreast of the field and in position to become a significant factor in the world videotex market.[27]

For the past few years, the world of videotex has waited for the United States to make its choice while the United States has waited for the videotex systems of the world to beat a path to its door. The path now is well-worn and there are signs that the giant U.S. market is ready to buy. What it buys, where it buys it, and how it employs it will have a decisive effect on the international development of videotex.

Development of videotex has been delayed in the United States partly because videotex systems were conceived originally as national public systems of computer communications on the British or French model. This concept is alien to the United States where communications of all kinds, including telephone and television, are owned and operated by commercial interests under state regulation. While comprehensive European videotex systems were being planned by state agencies, activity in the United States was limited to a few cautious trials by commercial media interests. In the meantime, the Federal Communications Commission, the central regulatory agency, started work on a regulatory framework for the new medium.

This incomplete structure already is vibrating with activity. A few years ago, the number of videotex trials in the United States could be numbered on the fingers of one hand. Now a computer would be needed to list and track them. It is difficult to find a large newspaper, publishing organization, or television network in the United States that is not involved in videotex. Major corporations from such other fields as banking, merchandising, and entertainment are now investing heavily. This sudden increase in videotex activity in the United States is the most important development for the medium since the British commitment in the 1970s. It is responsible for transforming the future of videotex from a matter for speculation to a subject of analysis.

The pattern of videotex development in the United States will be determined in this decade. It will affect videotex and perhaps many other commercial and cultural institutions in other countries, Canada in particular. At some point during this decade, the United States is expected to adopt a standard videotex system to prevent the development of rival, incompatible systems. Without a system of its own, the U.S. is now studying the merits of systems developed in Britain, France, and Canada. All three systems are involved in U.S. videotex trials at the moment.

Some notion of the size of the potential American market can be gained by contemplating American Telephone and Telegraph, the colossus that accounts for 80 per cent of the US $50 billion annual business of communications carriers in the United States. AT&T's largest rival is General Telephone and Electronics. Although GTE's revenues are only about 10 per cent of AT&T's, it is close to the British Post Office in terms of numbers of telephones installed.

AT&T is only one of many U.S. corporations now investing in videotex, but its activities are studied closely, not only because of its size but because decisions by the Federal Communications Commission affecting AT&T will set a pattern for the industry. The announcement by AT&T on May 20, 1981, that it intended to adopt videotex standards that may eventually become compatible with Canada's Telidon system, for instance, immediately created the prospect of incompatible North American and European systems.

In a joint venture with Knight-Ridder Newspapers, AT&T has been involved in a relatively modest videotex field trial in a Miami suburb, Coral Gables, since July, 1980. The first phase of the trial rotated 30 terminals around 160 homes. Although the number of terminals was small, the database was extensive, containing news and other information from Knight-Ridder's Miami *Herald*, the New York *Times*, Associated Press, and CBS Publications. It also offered teleshopping services for such advertisers as Sears Roebuck and J.C. Penny, as well as information from local advertisers. In the first phase of this trial, lasting about eight months, Knight-Ridder spent about US $2.5 million preparing and maintaining the database. AT&T provided the terminals and all technical services, which included running a new telephone line into every home selected for the trial and attaching it to a specially modified AT&T television set.[28]

Less publicized but more significant was AT&T's first trial of an electronic telephone directory in Albany, New York. AT&T's Electronic Information Service (EIS) supplied white and yellow pages telephone directory information to 83 homes. The corporation subsequently announced that it would extend this service to include classified advertising and consumer information in EIS II, a trial in Austin, Texas, that would service 680 homes and 60 businesses. In the Albany trial, AT&T provided only services, such as time, weather, and directory information, that it already was authorized to deliver in other forms, either in print or over the telephone. This shielded it from regulatory challenge. The additional services planned for Austin drew an immediate response from the Texas Daily Newspapers Association. The newspapers asked the Texas Public Utility Commission to stop AT&T from becoming a provider as well as a carrier of information.

This prospective dual role for AT&T is at the heart of a regulatory dispute that will dominate discussion about videotex in the U.S. in the near future. Katharine Graham, president of the Washington *Post* and the American Newspaper Publishers' Association, summarized the newspapers' objections in 1980, when she said, "The possibility of one giant corporation becoming the information supplier ... to four out of five American households strikes many of us as profoundly troubling."[29] While U.S. newspaper publishers as a group endorse the principle of carrier-content separation, a growing number of American newspapers are violating it in practice by acquiring ownership of cable TV systems as quickly as they can, motivated partly by the prospect of news and advertising competition from on-screen print.

In Florida, AT&T used an alpha-mosaic videotex system similar to Prestel. Second in size to AT&T, GTE began testing a version of Prestel in the United States in 1979. In October, 1980, it moved in a new direction by announcing its own interactive videotex system based on Telidon, a technology familiar to GTE's Canadian subsidiary, B.C. Telephone. At the outset, GTE attempted to avoid confrontation with newspapers by offering local videotex franchises to newspapers. Under GTE's *Infovision* system, local newspapers would operate the system with GTE supplying the equipment, including an initial base of 2,000 terminals. Local information would be supplied by the newspapers and national news by GTE's *Telenet*, an existing packet-switched data network for computer communications. Local advertising revenues would stay with the local newspapers while GTE would receive revenue from national advertising.

Among the U.S. television networks, CBS has been the most active in teletext. In July, 1980, after technical tests for one and a half years, it recommended Antiope to the FCC as a teletext standard. The following November, it announced a field trial using two stations in Los Angeles, one CBS-owned and the other non-commercial (*KCET*). This trial was to begin in 1981 with 100 decoder-equipped receivers rotated through private homes and public locations. Antiope's promoters in France are reported to be supplying equipment and technical assistance worth more than US $1 million.

A number of individual TV stations have experimented with teletext in recent years. Since 1978, *KSL-TV* in Salt Lake City has broadcast several hundred pages of teletext using a system developed by Texas Instruments. *KSL-TV* also has tested a hybrid system which it calls "touch-tone teletext" that uses the phone connection in the home to access computer-stored information which is then broadcast to the home TV set. The Public Broadcasting System, using station *WETA* in Washington and 60 Telidon terminals, is involved in an early consumer trial of teletext. Information will be supplied by the Washington *Post*, public libraries, the Smithsonian Institution, several U.S. government agencies, and other IPs. Other teletext trials are planned by stations in Florida, California, and in Chicago, using Ceefax technology and broadcasting information from newspapers and news services as well as from other sources.

Trials of interactive cable TV in the U.S. preceded tests of videotex and teletext. The now-famous QUBE system in Columbus, Ohio, is a two-way cable TV system in place since December, 1977. A joint venture of American Express and Warner Communications Inc., it has 30,000 subscribers who have used it to indicate political or program preferences, to shop, and to receive three categories of TV programming, conventional broadcast TV, pay TV, and community TV, each category having 10 channels. QUBE has not provided videotex but in January, 1981, it offered a small number of its subscribers the computer information services of Compuserve, a data processing service owned by H. & R. Block which has commercial clients in 260 cities but also provides a number of computer services to the growing home market.

Many other companies in the expanding cable TV market are testing interactive systems, including Rogers Cablesystems Ltd., a Canadian company with a franchise in Portland, Oregon. Rogers is including a Telidon system in the package of services that it assembles when bidding for U.S. franchises. Generally, in the current competition for urban cable TV franchises in the U.S., contenders now are offering interactive systems with some form of videotex services.

These systems are an outgrowth of the textual information that cable TV services have transmitted for years — a primitive form of teletext without any selection capability by viewers. About 40 per cent of the more than 4,000 cable TV systems in the U.S. now carry this form of on-screen print supplied by Reuters (*News-View*), Associated Press (*Newscable*), or United Press International (*Cable Newswire*). About 300 cable systems now receive Reuters' *Monitor* via satellite. This improved service was launched early in 1979 and enables viewers to select and "freeze" pages of information by using a keypad.

Developing alongside videotex and teletext in the U.S., but still separate from them, the home computer market has flourished without regulatory guidance. As the price of computers has decreased and as more services have been available to the home enthusiast, this market has grown rapidly.

The first home computers were offered for sale in 1975. The number in U.S. homes had grown to an estimated 450,000 by the end of 1980, and was expected to exceed 1,000,000 by 1983 as hardware prices continue to decline.[30]

Up to now, on-line computer services have been viewed as distinctive from videotex. They have been expensive and relatively complicated, designed for the specialist user rather than the mass market. A typical on-line service provider, in this case one of the world's largest, is the non-profit Ohio College Library Centre's *Channel 2000*. This national computer network for libraries contained 5,500,000 entries in 1979. Recently, the gap between specialist systems such as this and public videotex has started to narrow. Channel 2000, for instance, is involved in a videotex experiment in Columbus, Ohio, that supplies library, encyclopedia, and banking information to 200 home users. The test is financed, in part, by an innovative local bank. As the providers of information test the home market, home computer services are exploring new sources of information for their growing lists of subscribers.

In 1979, Source Telecomputing Corporation began to offer access to its computers to owners of personal computers as well as to corporations. In 1980, it reported 8,000 users of which 80 per cent were home users. They were able to access such databases as the New York *Times*, UPI News Services, travel information, financial and accounting packages, a directory of users, classified ads, bulletin board, electronic mail, and games. Teleshopping is possible with the "Comp-U-Card" service. In 1980, *Readers' Digest* purchased a majority interest in the company.

Compuserve, originally created to sell data processing to corporations, launched Compuserve Information Services in 1980 to exploit the growing home market. Its list of services includes a reference encyclopedia entitled "news and family information", electronic mail, a national bulletin board, securities information, personal finance information and games. Compuserve, owned by H. & R. Block, has agreements with computer hardware retailers such as Tandy, Atari, and Radio Shack to market its information services. Its recent agreement with Meredith Publishers, owners of *Better Homes and Gardens*, *Farming*, and other periodicals, illustrates its continuing search for new sources of information. Compuserve claimed to have 5,000 users in 1980, 95 per cent of them using personal computers at home to access the service.

This thriving home computer market is a distinctive American development which already is influencing videotex in the United States. In Europe, where the market for small computers or "microcomputers" has been only 10 to 20 per cent of that in the United States, videotex is being established generally under state communications monopolies. It is the state-owned carrier that organizes the service, promotes it, and provides it with a corporate identity. In the United States, videotex is being developed and promoted by a variety of participants — telephone companies, television networks, newspapers, and magazine publishers, as well as the manufacturers of computer equipment and programs.

The European pattern indicates that videotex there will continue to be identifiable as distinct national services, at least in this decade. Standards will be set by national governments. Trans-border connections between these national systems will involve lengthy technical and political discussions. In the United States, and perhaps in Canada to a lesser extent, the definition of videotex and its structure in future are blurred by the approaching convergence of videotex and home computer systems. At present, home computers cannot be used as videotex terminals, but it is estimated that already there are 40,000 home computers in the U.S. that could be equipped to access electronic publishing services with only minor adaptation. An estimated 10,000 personal computer users in the U.S. already participate in some form of electronic publishing service or other videotex-like service from their homes.[31] The blurring of the distinction between home computers and videotex is peculiar to the development of videotex in the North American market and of special interest to Canada, where the federal government has taken a "European" role in the promotion of videotex within an "American" economy that already is an important market for home computers and computer services from the United States.

With a creative society and a wealthy economy, the United States is the only country in the world that can afford the luxury of true competition in the development of a new communications medium such as videotex. While other nations have had to make early commitments to specific videotex systems, thereby locking themselves into systems and structures that may be difficult to change, the United States, up to a point, can afford duplication of effort among many competitors in the private sector. It can delay making commitments until systems have been tested extensively by public and commercial corporations searching for the elusive fulcrum between quality of content and technology, on one side of the balance, and profit on the other. Possessing the richest consumer market in the world, it can afford to let the market decide.

This process is now under way in the United States. This decade, presumably, will see decisions there on the viability of videotex as a mass medium, on videotex standards, on the structure of videotex systems, and on regulatory issues related to publishing on videotex and freedom of the press. Whatever happens in the United States on all these questions will affect all other nations, Canada first and foremost.

References

1. Charles Dalfen, *Regulatory Aspects of the New Technology*. Research study for the Royal Commission on Newspapers, 1981. Appendix I. Public Archives.
2. Roger Woolfe, *Videotex*. London, Heyden and Son, 1980. p. 107.
3. Ibid., p. 106.
4. Interviews with Rex Winsbury, Fintel, London, February, 1981.
5. "Teletext: TV Gets Married to the Printed Word." *Broadcasting*, August, 20, 1979. p. 33.
6. Woolfe, *Videotex*, p. 105.
7. Interviews with Rex Winsbury, London, February, 1981.
8. Ibid.
9. Interviews with Prestel executives, London, February, 1981.
10. Ibid.
11. Michael L. Ford, "Marketing, Policy and Future Trends for Viewdata Services." Abstract of a 1979 speech.
12. P. McC. Montague, "The Electronic Newspaper". Online Conferences Ltd., 1980.
13. John Foxton, interview in Birmingham, February, 1981.
14. Report Two. Communications Studies and Planning International, in *Context*, New York: March, 1980.
15. Interview with Prestel executives, London, February, 1981.
16. Sir John Barrow, "Electronic Publishing and the Government". Online Conferences Ltd., 1980.

17. John Howkins, "The Information Societies." *In Search*, 7(2), Spring, 1980 p. 14.
18. John C. LeGates, "Changes in the Information Industries." Speech to the Board of Directors of the American Newspaper Publishers Association. September 11, 1980. p. 5.
19. François-Régis Hutin, quoted in "Presse régionale: le défi télématique." *l'Express*, December 13, 1980. p. 85.
20. Interviews with telecommunications officials, both public and private sectors, in Paris, February, 1981.
21. Ibid.
22. Ibid.
23. Interviews and tour of teletext production facilities, Bonn and Cologne, February, 1981.
24. Christopher Evans, *The Mighty Micro*. London, Victor Gollancz, 1979. p. 93.
25. Iann Barron and Ray Curnow, *The Future of Microelectronics*. London, Frances, 1979. p. 202.
26. Ibid., p. 203.
27. Information provided by Communications Studies and Planning International, New York.
28. Interviews with Viewdata Corporation of America, Inc., in Miami, January, 1981.
29. Quoted in "The new electronic newsboy," Boston *Sunday Globe*, August 31, 1980.
30. Information provided by Communications Studies and Planning International, New York.
31. Ibid.

6
Telidon

Videotex development in Canada probably would have followed the pattern of smaller European countries, using British or French technology, had it not been for the invention of Telidon within the Department of Communications in 1978. Telidon is a second-generation coding system for videotex which facilitates the production and display of highly refined graphics. At this point in the rapidly evolving history of videotex, it is technically the best videotex system on the market but it may not be the most cost-efficient.

Like Prestel, Telidon was invented incidentally by a research engineer who had set out to devise something quite different. Herbert G. Bown's original assignment in Ottawa, after joining the Defence Research Telecommunications Establishment in 1966, had been to develop an "electronic blackboard" that would function through a conventional telephone system. Unlike the earlier "picturephone" in the U.S. and Britain, the "blackboard" designed by Bown and others transmitted not photographic images but diagrams produced by computers or drawn by "electronic pens" during transmission. This was developed in Canada originally as a means of communicating military information.

When this defence work was absorbed in 1971 by the new Department of Communications, Bown continued his work on the transmission of computer graphics by telephone line, as a member of DOC's Communications Research Centre. Several systems were developed for military and civilian use. The CRC developments were primarily in software, related to the concepts and computer programs which allowed graphics to be easily created and efficiently transmitted. In 1976, a technology transfer agreement was signed with a small electronics manufacturer near Ottawa, Norpak Ltd., for the development and sale of commercial graphics terminals based on CRC technology.

About the same time, officials at DOC became aware of the rapid development of Prestel and Antiope videotex systems overseas. In 1977, the Communications Research Centre was asked to build a replica of the Prestel system. In four days, the system was simulated and demonstrated but the manager of the laboratory, Herb Bown, was heard to mutter something about not designing a videotex system that way, if he had been asked to start from scratch. He was asked, and in a short time Bown perfected and demonstrated his idea of a better system.

By mid-1978, there were reports that Canadian telephone, broadcasting, and cable TV companies were adopting or purchasing British and French systems for videotex field trials in Canada. In order to make them aware of the development within DOC, "Canadian Videotex", as it then was called, was demonstrated publicly for the first time at a press conference on August 15, 1978. Almost immediately, Canada established itself as one of the leading Western nations, along with Britain and France, in the development of videotex technology. Since then, Prestel, Antiope, and Telidon have competed for international acceptance.

The heart of Telidon is its unique Picture Description Instructions, a computer code or "shorthand" to assemble the elements of a graphic image on a television screen. In the earlier alpha-mosaic systems, the operator of a page-creating terminal created an image on the screen square by square, laboriously picking out the co-ordinates in a mosaic grid to fill in squares with different colors. Newer editing aids have simplified and speeded up this process without altering its basic design. With Telidon, an alpha-geometric system, an operator, by pushing a few buttons, can instruct the system to build up an image using basic geometric elements — point, line, arc, polygon, and rectangle. The difference is apparent immediately. Prestel creates a graphic image line by line, from top to bottom of the screen. Telidon's more detailed images take shape in various areas of the screen, as if they were being sketched quickly by hand.

Because the Picture Description Instructions are abbreviated and relatively simple, fewer bits of information are needed to compose an image. Less storage and transmission capacity is required. Unlike some earlier systems, Telidon isn't limited by the capacity of the display system. Inexpensive, low-resolution Telidon videotex terminals can display images in response to the same transmission that activates a high-resolution set. The only difference is in picture quality. The cheaper set, unable to fully utilize the Telidon code, displays an inferior, Prestel-type image. Telidon also has the ability to superimpose images and to transmit animated images. The system can be used to display photographic images, as can the other systems, but this requires the transmission of too many bits of information within a limited period of time to make it practical at the moment.

Officials of the Department of Communications have stated that "the technical superiority of Telidon is not contested," [1] but the system does have its critics, mainly because of its cost. It has been called the "Cadillac" of videotex, too expensive for the mass market, while the first-generation alpha-mosaic systems have been said to provide a good and reliable "Volkswagen" service. This impression was confirmed by the cost of early Telidon terminals. The Mark I terminals built for the first technical trials by Norpak sold in 1979 for $3,500, including a slightly modified Electrohome color TV set. Without the TV set, the cost was $2,600.

The most common modification of a color TV set for videotex, not always understood by viewers watching demonstrations for the first time, is to direct the videotex signal directly to the color "guns" inside the set that produce combinations of red, blue, and green. This RGB route produces a dramatically superior image compared with the product of a signal sent via RF — the usual antenna input. Most European sets have external input jacks for RGB but in North America most sets have what is known as a "hot chassis" design which cannot accommodate an RGB jack. This means that most existing North American sets can receive videotex only via RF, which limits graphic detail and the range of color.

By the spring of 1980, the cost of a color Telidon terminal able to receive RGB had dropped to about $1,200. DOC officials, claiming that this price range was competitive with Prestel and Antiope equipment, held out the promise of further reductions, to the $250 to $400 range for terminal equipment, excluding the cost of the TV set, when third-generation terminals are mass-produced.

At this time, however, high-resolution Telidon that exploits the full potential of its unique system remains more expensive than standard Prestel or Antiope equipment. Low-resolution Telidon — in theory, because it does not exist on the market — is competitive with the other systems in terms of cost. In other words, for the same money you can get the same quality of image on all three systems but only Telidon provides the option of upgrading to a more refined image, using the same database and signal. No one knows, at this time, which grade of image consumers will find best, in relation to cost.

The invention of Telidon in a federal government laboratory radically altered the Canadian approach to videotex. Before Telidon, only a few telephone, television, and cable TV companies were experimenting on a small scale with British and French videotex systems. Official interest was almost non-existent. After Telidon was announced in 1978, the federal government became its chief promoter. In less than three years, Canada became one of the most active participants internationally in the development of videotex.

"If we in Canada work together and act quickly, we can be in the forefront of interactive television technology," Jeanne Sauvé, then minister of communications, forecast when Telidon was announced in 1978.[2] Less than a year later, in April, 1979, she announced a federal commitment of $9 million to a four-year program to develop Telidon, stating that it was "the best technology of its kind in the world" and that it had "the potential for creating thousands of jobs for Canadians in the manufacturing and service supply industries".[3] The money was designated for three main areas of activity: field trials, development of Telidon hardware, and related activities such as co-ordination and standardization.

Less than two years later, Ottawa announced that it already had invested more than $12,600,000 in Telidon and intended to commit an additional $27,500,000 to be spent in the following two years. Again, the economic return on this investment was cited as the main reason for making it. "We are convinced that Telidon is quite simply the best videotex system in the world," said Francis Fox, who had succeeded Mme Sauvé as minister of communications. "We believe that Telidon will be a key piece in the vast new information industries of multi-billion dollar scale providing thousands of knowledge-intensive jobs in Canada." Fox assigned the new funds primarily to subsidize the purchase of 6,000 Telidon terminals by the industry "for the start of operational systems or the conduct of market trials," to complete the development of VLSI (very large scale integrated) low-cost terminals, to help the launching of a national broadcast teletext service in English and French, to support market development, and to foster "public interest initiatives to permit disadvantaged groups lacking resources ... to exploit the Telidon potential as a communications medium".[4]

Despite the increased funding, DOC's Telidon Development Program is still scheduled to terminate in 1983. That remains the date when further development of Telidon is supposed to be entrusted to private industry.

Within a remarkably short time, Telidon has become an important part of international videotex development. In late 1980, Telidon was ratified as a world videotex standard, alongside the Prestel and Antiope systems, by the International Telegraph and Telephone Consultative Committee of the International Telecommunications Union, an agency of the United Nations. In 1981, Canadian work on standards was focused on the Federal Communications Commission in the United States, already studying a request for adoption of Antiope as a standard from the CBS television network. Telidon's first penetration of the U.S. market occurred in 1980 when the Corporation for Public Broadcasting chose the Canadian system over British and French systems for a field trial in Washington, D.C. Another sale was made in Venezuela where Telidon was selected for a government information service that will place videotex terminals in public places in the capital city of Caracas. Telidon was included in services listed in several cable TV franchises awarded to joint American-Canadian ventures. In Canada, all field trials of videotex by 1981 were committed to using Telidon, although not always exclusively.

Despite this early activity, the large government investment in Telidon remains speculative. There is still uncertainty about the future of videotex itself. If videotex expands as a new medium, Telidon is only one of three systems now available. Even if Telidon becomes the predominant system, the economic impact on Canada's electronics industry is hard to predict, partly because of the nature of Telidon itself.

There is widespread misunderstanding of Telidon among the Canadian public, some of it fostered by the government, abetted by an uncritical press. Much of the official publicity about Telidon has focused on its importance for the future of Canada's electronic industry. The impression has been created that Telidon resembles the CANDU nuclear reactor developed by Canada, in the sense that it is a machine or apparatus exclusively available in Canada.

Telidon is not at all like this, a point made clear at the outset of its development. In 1979, John C. Madden, then director general of Special Research Programs for the Department of Communications, described Telidon as "first and foremost a communications protocol, a way of storing and transmitting graphical and other information with a high degree of efficiency. As such, it is not patentable.

"Anyone can take the published specifications for the Picture Description Instructions (or PDIs) which are at the heart of Telidon and develop a Telidon system," Madden explained. "All it takes is time and money, neither of which are required in very large quantities by modern industrial standards. The necessary expertise exists in many laboratories around the world."[5]

Dr. Madden explained that the decision by DOC to release information about Telidon's PDIs in 1978, as part of its effort to have Telidon accepted as an international standard, had been difficult. "In the end," he said, "we decided that the penalties of silence (which could have resulted in the adoption of an inferior world standard) were worse than the loss of lead time which resulted from revealing our methods."

The loss of competitive advantage was significant. "At this time," said Dr. Madden in the spring of 1979, "we have about a year of lead time over direct foreign competition — and make no mistake that there will be foreign competition. We understand that work has started in at least two foreign laboratories already, and we might normally expect to be among the last to know."[6]

Within a year, Madden's own knowledge of Telidon became available to researchers outside the country when he left DOC to become president of Microtel Pacific Research, the research arm of B.C. Telephone Company, itself a subsidiary of GTE in the United States.

In 1980, referring to the publication of Telidon's PDIs in 1978, Bernard Ostry, then deputy minister of communications in Ottawa, stated that "a competent software group could develop Telidon software from that description in 12 to 24 months."[7]

With Telidon's basic technology in the public domain, the federal government moved to transfer it to private industry as quickly as possible. Norpak Ltd., already licensed to use DOC-developed technology for commercial graphics terminals, acquired a licence to produce the first Telidon terminals. Other small electronics companies in the Ottawa region's embryonic network of high-technology industries also became active in Telidon research and production, along with a few companies in western Canada. Some of the companies are growing rapidly. Mitel Corporation, for instance, founded only in 1973, achieved sales of $43,000,000 in 1979 — but they are hardly in a position to meet sudden large export orders for Telidon hardware. Canada has only two electronics manufacturers capable of doing this: Northern Telecom, Bell Canada's manufacturing affiliate, and Electrohome Ltd., of Kitchener, Ontario. Both are heavily involved in Telidon. Northern Telecom is developing and supplying equipment for Bell's Telidon field trials in Ontario and Québec, the largest trials in the country; Electrohome is making Telidon terminals and expects Telidon sales in 1981 to be about $3,000,000, rising to $25,000,000 in 1982.

This activity to date has responded to demands of the Canadian market, massively stimulated by government investment. The likelihood of international sales of hardware remains unknown. Because of the public nature of Telidon's technology, adoption of Telidon by the United States or other countries would not give the Canadian electronics and videotex industries exclusive markets. At best, it would place them in a preferred position to exploit these new markets, because of their know-how and lead in development and manufacturing. Although Telidon may not be CANDU, its backers claim that it could do for the Canadian videotex and electronics industries what Volvo did for the Swedish automobile industry.

In Canada, there is no uncertainty about the initial impact of Telidon. Before the discovery of Telidon in 1978, Canada was an unremarkable participant in the development of videotex. When the federal government became the principal supporter of Telidon, it stimulated every aspect of videotex development. Within a few years, videotex field trials in Canada probably were more extensive than those in any other country.

References

1. John Madden, *Videotex in Canada*. Ottawa, Department of Communications, 1979. p. 22.
2. Canada. Department of Communications, News Release, August 15, 1978.

3. Jeanne Sauvé, Notes for an Address to the Canadian Cable Television Association, Toronto, April 2, 1979.
4. Francis Fox, Notes for Remarks on the Augmented Telidon Program, Ottawa, February 6, 1981.
5. Madden, *Videotex in Canada*, p. 26-27.
6. Ibid.
7. Bernard Ostry, "The Role of Government". *Inside Videotex*. Proceedings of a seminar, March, 1980. Toronto, Infomart, 1980, p. 50.

7
Videotex: Canadian field trials

Videotex development in Canada resembles neither the state-directed programs of England or France nor the competitive free-for-all in the United States. It is, characteristically, somewhere in between.

The largest single investor is the federal government. The other major avenues of state investment in videotex are publicly-owned telephone companies, which sponsor videotex trials in some provinces, and television networks. Both the Canadian Broadcasting Corporation and TV Ontario are experimenting with teletext using Telidon. In the private sector, telephone companies in some provinces, like those in the United States, have been major developers of videotex, along with newspaper groups, cable TV companies, and broadcasters.

In May, 1981, there were 12 Telidon field trials listed in Canada. Three were operational. Six were scheduled to begin service before the end of the year and three in 1982. An international trial of Telidon also had been announced. As in other countries, most trials were behind schedule because of difficulties in obtaining equipment and creating databases. Creating videotex pages has been more time-consuming and expensive than expected. Information banks for the early trials have been incomplete and unsophisticated, discouraging some users. Despite the heavy federal investment since 1978, a survey in February, 1981, revealed that only 338 Telidon terminals actually were in operation, 267 being used for videotex trials and 71 for teletext broadcast by television networks.[1] Because of the small number of terminals in most trials, the inadequacy of information banks, weaknesses in statistical data, and the absence of market conditions — terminals and information are provided free in most trials — the current set of trials will not produce firm conclusions about the commercial future of videotex.

Even as the initial trials went into operation, supplying information primarily to terminals in homes, experience in England seemed to show that residential services would not be viable in the near future. The French had decided, in making their deep plunge into videotex, that field trials were often a waste of time. This policy was expressed at a Toronto videotex conference in 1980 by Pierre Gaujard, president of

Antiope Videotex Systems Inc., the Washington company formed in 1979 to promote Antiope in the United States. Said Mr. Gaujard:

> "Taking part in any development testing with the idea of just dipping your toes in the water and writing it all off as an R&D expense, come what may, runs the very real risk of producing only wet toes and a nice little report titled 'Results of Videotex Field Trials', and discouragement at not being much closer to answering the question 'how do I make money with this?' than you were before the experiment began."[2]

Canadian field trials in the spring of 1981 seemed to confirm what Gordon Thompson of Bell-Northern Research had written about "technology and the information society" a year earlier: "All the excitement is in the expectation; the reality is really quite disappointing."[3] Visions of the wired city were fading quickly. Canadian entrepreneurs, engineers, bureaucrats, computer programmers, writers, artists, and others involved in the videotex trials were discovering how wide the gap is between theory and practice, between vision and reality. Many costly mistakes were being made. The press releases of the early prophets were looking more and more utopian. At the same time, lessons were being learned. Within the unco-ordinated patchwork of field trials across Canada, hundreds of Canadians were gaining valuable experience in building and operating the basic systems of the information society. If that is the direction in which mankind is headed, the money and effort being spent on the field trials was being well invested, regardless of the future of Telidon. The ultimate importance of Telidon, in fact, may lie in its role as a catalyst of videotex development in Canada.

Before Telidon was announced in August, 1978, videotex development in Canada was limited to a small program within Bell Canada. The company had followed closely the evolution of videotex in England and France and had started in 1977 to plan a Canadian service, aiming at offering a full-scale service to the public in 1982-83. Bell's videotex, at that time, was based on modified Prestel technology. Its plans were made public in 1978, almost coincidentally with the Department of Communications' announcement of its new technology.

At first, Bell decided to test both British and Canadian technologies, with Prestel as the main system. In the spring of 1979, Bell was still planning a Prestel-type system, using computers at centralized "videotex service centres" at the outset, evolving later into a decentralized or "gateway" network giving access to outside computers. Bell planners at this stage were planning to connect their system to information providers in the United States through existing computer-communications networks, Telenet and Tymnet in the United States and Datapac in Canada. The American connection was dropped, for the time being, when Bell adopted Telidon exclusively for its field trials. At that time, early in 1980, only British and French technologies were being considered in the United States and neither Prestel nor Antiope are compatible with Telidon.

Bell's trial of *Vista*, the name of its Telidon videotex service, is the largest of the Canadian trials and the most important of the seven videotex trials operated or planned by Canadian telephone companies. Like most of the trials, the Vista trial is a little later and a little smaller than originally planned. Early in 1980, it was described as a $10,000,000 venture that would involve 1,000 residential and business telephone subscribers, mostly in the Toronto area. The trial originally was scheduled to start by 1981 after installation of terminals in 1980.

After going through what Bell executives described in 1980 as "an agonizing exercise on that subject", Bell initially decided to restrict the trial to Ontario subscribers, without testing it in Québec among French-speaking subscribers.[4] Apparently the subject was reopened within a short time and Québec was included in the trial. By February, 1981, the budget had climbed to $11,000,000 and the number of terminals had dropped to 490 — 300 in Toronto households, 80 in Cap Rouge, a small community on the outskirts of Québec City, and the remainder for use in public places and institutions, and as demonstration models in Montréal and the Ottawa/Hull region.

Vista was demonstrated at an international videotex conference in Toronto in May, 1981. Regular service would begin later in the year. The objective was to create a database or information bank of 75,000 pages by the end of 1981, 15,000 in French. Information providers include TV Ontario, Dominion Stores, Infomart (a joint venture of Southam Inc. and Torstar Corporation), the Ontario government, *Le Soleil*, the Consumers' Association of Canada, and Télé-Direct, Bell's own "yellow pages" publishing subsidiary. Télé-Direct not only will publish "electronic yellow pages" for Bell during the field trial, but also offer its services as an editor and creator of videotex material to other information providers. There will be classified and retail advertising on Vista; teleshopping and telebanking will be tested in 1982.

The index of material on Vista will be prepared by Bell; the telephone company also will record data on use of the system. Both these activities could be in conflict with current legislation that limits Bell's role to the carrying of communications regardless of content.

Smaller than Bell Canada but perhaps more adventurous in exploring videotex is the publicly-owned Manitoba Telephone System (MTS). It has undertaken three field trials, including the first videotex trial to become operational in Canada. Project Ida, named after Ida Kates who became Manitoba's first female telephone operator in 1882, started in April, 1980, with transmission of educational videotapes. Telidon was added in June, 1980. Information services, security alarms, and utilities metering are also part of the $1,500,000 trial which began officially in March, 1981. The host computer in Winnipeg serves 37 Telidon terminals, 30 of them in homes in South Headingley, seven miles from downtown Winnipeg.

Project Ida differs from Vista in a number of respects. Transmission is by means of coaxial cable rather than the telephone system. By using cable, owned by the Manitoba Telephone System, Ida can deliver a wider range of services than Vista, including conventional telephone service and television as well as two types of videotex for trial purposes.

In addition to Telidon, Project Ida will test an American-designed videotex service called *Omnitex*. In the spring of 1980, Mike Aysan, manager of product development for MTS, explained the difference between the two services at a videotex conference in Toronto: "Omnitex can achieve a $100 per subscriber objective. Telidon? Today it's at $1,200. It was at $3,700 eighteen months ago. I've heard numbers recently around $300 forecast within the next 24 months. If that's the case, there's still a gap between Omnitex and Telidon of $200. Another feature of Omnitex is a full English keyboard ... It's not a plot against Telidon," stated Mr.

Aysan. "We wholeheartedly support the Canadian dream called 'Telidon'. It's just our bit of insurance."[5]

In 1980, the Winnipeg *Tribune* became the first Canadian newspaper to supply videotex news on a daily schedule. It provided local, national, and international news, sports, financial data, and an entertainment package, about 20 pages in all, updated daily. The service was provided through Infomart, operators of the host computer for Ida. No comparable news service has been part of Ida since August, 1980, when Southam closed the Winnipeg *Tribune*.

The database for Project Ida has grown slowly. In February, 1981, it contained only 4,000 pages, less than half the projected total. The inadequate database was blamed for lack of sustained interest by some of the participants in Ida. According to an MTS official, many of them have shown little interest in continuing the experiment. Infomart already has decided that such a field trial of less than 100 terminals does not provide useful data on the potential consumer market for videotex. MTS is working on plans to expand the test to include 1,000 homes.

Manitoba Telephone System also is involved in building a $6,000,000 rural fibre optical system to service 150 homes and businesses in the small town of Elie, 25 miles west of Winnipeg. MTS will pay $1,000,000, but the major portion of funding will come from the Department of Communications and the Canadian Telecommunication Carriers' Association. By mid-1981, the high-capacity fibre optical lines, according to the MTS schedule, was to carry telephone service, nine-channel cable TV, and seven-channel FM radio. Interactive Telidon would be added later in the year, using the Infomart computer in Winnipeg.

The third field trial involving MTS is Project Grassroots, described by Communications Minister Francis Fox in November, 1980, as "the world's first commercial Telidon service".[6] Project Grassroots, also operated by Infomart from its Winnipeg computer, will supply agricultural information to farmers. The service was to begin in 1981 with 25 demonstration terminals in such places as the offices of provincial agricultural representatives, grain terminals, and community centres. Later, 25 terminals will be placed on private farms. Terminals on Elie's fibre optical system also will be able to receive Grassroots information. Grassroots is the only trial that will use MTS telephone lines. Farms with terminals will have new lines connected to their homes so that the trial will not interfere with ordinary telephone service.

Before committing itself to Grassroots, MTS commissioned a survey of Manitoba farmers to assess their information needs. The study showed that 75 per cent of the farmers were satisfied with the quality of information they were receiving, primarily from daily newspapers and weekly publications for farmers. Of the 25 per cent who felt that information was incomplete, almost 40 per cent believed that a videotex service could be very useful. This response was considered to be sufficiently strong to warrant an investment of $1,500,000 by Infomart in the compilation of a videotex database for Grassroots which eventually could serve a market of 3,000 farmers in southern Manitoba.

At the end of April, 1981, the New Brunswick Telephone Company became the second Canadian telephone utility to inaugurate a videotex service. Project Mercury, in the Millidgeville area of Saint John, eventually will supply Telidon and alarm services via coaxial cable to 45 terminals which will be rotated through 75 homes, businesses, and community institutions. Information providers listed for the service include the local daily newspaper, the *Telegraph Journal/Evening Times Globe*, which will supply news, weather, sports, and entertainment.

B.C. Telephone's trial, scheduled to start late in 1981 with 125 Telidon terminals, is the only one directed primarily at commercial use rather than the home market. B.C. Tel, at least in the initial stage, is preparing the database, the index of services that will be part of the database, and a printed directory or "users' guide". Dominion Directories, B.C. Tel's "yellow pages" subsidiary, will be a major information provider.

Alberta Government Telephones was reported in 1980 to be planning a Telidon field trial using 150 terminals in Calgary. The trial originally was scheduled to start by the end of 1980, but early in 1981 AGT was reassessing its plans and studying a number of different options for a trial starting later in the year.

One cable TV company, Télécâble Vidéotron in suburban Montréal, has announced an ambitious $4,500,000 plan to connect its own host computer to 250 Telidon terminals in homes of subscribers. The company has listed news, weather, sports, videogames, entertainment listings, classified ads, real estate listings, yellow pages, alarm services, and remote utility meter-reading among its projected services, but the target date for starting videotex service is April, 1983.

In Saskatchewan, Cablecom Corporation, a telecommunications company financed largely by co-operatives, has announced tentative plans for a videotex field trial starting some time after 1982, focused primarily on commercial use.

In addition to participating in Telidon field trials by telephone and cable TV companies, the federal government is organizing its own $1,500,000 trial to supply information about government services to Telidon terminals in government offices and public places across the country. The trial was scheduled to start in the spring of 1981 but encountered delays. The network may eventually include up to 700 terminals served by host computers in Ottawa and Winnipeg. Information is being supplied by government departments and by a "Task Force on Service to the Public". DOC has contracted out the formatting of videotex material to Infomart.

Telidon also is the system used for two Canadian teletext trials. In January, 1980, the Ontario Educational Communications Authority (TV Ontario) launched a teletext trial, using broadcast transmission and telephone lines, designed to serve 55 terminals. In February, 1981, only 15 Telidon terminals were in the field. For an immature system, with a small annual budget of $450,000, the TV Ontario trial has enjoyed an extraordinary amount of publicity, because of its pioneering character.

The first extensive trial of teletext is being planned by the Canadian Broadcasting Corporation. The CBC announced in June, 1980, that it would study the use of teletext using Telidon. At the same time, it became a member of the Videotex Information Service Providers Association of Canada (VISPAC), a trade association of several hundred information providers. The CBC envisages trials in English and French with 250 terminals in the Montréal area and 150 each in the Toronto and Calgary areas; they were expected to start late in 1981 or in 1982, but no date has been announced. Information on CBC teletext would include news, weather, and sports, financial and consumer information, program schedules for radio and television with supplementary information about programs, travel and hotel information, horoscopes and games. The CBC also intends to investigate the commercial potential of videotex during the trials, including the possibility of supporting regular TV commercials with lists of local retail outlets or information about sales that could be updated daily. The trials might help to resolve questions about union jurisdictions and the new technology. There are also technical difficulties to overcome related to transmitting teletext, which is for immediate viewing, in combination with conventional TV signals that are time-delayed for staggered local use in different time zones across the country.

An international videotex trial using Telidon was to begin in 1981, according to an announcement by Teleglobe Canada, the Crown agency in charge of overseas telecommunications. Terminals and software for the three-year project will be supplied by Infomart under a $1,100,000 contract with Teleglobe. Total cost of the project was estimated at $4,100,000. Teleglobe stated that its objective was a database of up to 100,000 pages. There was no indication of the number of terminals involved or where they would be placed.[7] The Teleglobe project will be in competition with Prestel International, Britain's international videotex service. Commenting on the Teleglobe announcement, Communications Minister Francis Fox said that the project would contribute to Telidon's use in other countries.

In Canada, as in the United States, videotex trials are occurring at the same time as other developments in communications for homes and businesses that eventually may influence the future of videotex.

While telephone companies collaborate with the Department of Communications in Telidon field trials, cable TV companies have moved ahead on their own to introduce two-way or interactive commercial service. The pioneer in these explorations of a new market is Rogers Cablesystems Inc., formerly Canadian Cablesystems, one of the largest cable TV companies in the world with franchises in Canada, the United States, and the United Kingdom. In 1979, Canadian Cablesystems introduced the first interactive cable TV in Canada in London, Ontario. During discussions of the 1980 merger between Canadian Cablesystems Ltd., of Toronto, and Premier Communications Ltd., of Vancouver, that led to the creation of Rogers Cablesystems Inc., Canadian Cablesystems outlined plans to the Canadian Radio-television and Telecommunications Commission (CRTC) to install an interactive system in Vancouver capable of serving 10,000 Telidon terminals. The estimated cost of this system was $12,000,000.

In 1979, Ted Rogers, then president of Canadian Cablesystems, estimated that it would take five years and $800,000,000 to convert all 3,700,000 Canadian homes served by cable to the new technology.

In 1978, the CRTC encouraged Canadian cable TV companies to investigate new ways of using their systems by stating that it would give "prompt and favorable consideration to applications by cable television licensees for the use of their systems to provide new communication services of a non-programming nature."[8] Rogers Cablesystems responded in 1981 by proposing a package of interactive services to the CRTC that would include security surveillance systems for homes and businesses, subscriber opinion polling, energy meter reading, automatic measurement of TV viewing habits with the consent of subscribers, video games, teleshopping, news and information, and shared computer services providing access to national computing services in the United States. In March, 1981, Rogers Cablesystems asked the CRTC for permission to provide this package to its cable subscribers in Toronto and 11 other urban areas in Ontario.

In November, 1980, the international communications periodical *Intermedia* reported that Canadian Cablesystems, as it then was called, "will probably work alongside Southam Inc., the newspaper chain which now has a practical monopoly in Vancouver" in planning the introduction of Telidon to its subscribers. As *Intermedia* noted, "the combination of CCL and Southam in a city with an average cable penetration of 70 per cent would be a powerful one."[9]

For Ted Rogers, president of Rogers Cablesystems, the outline of the looming confrontation with the telephone companies for the provision of interactive videotex is clear. "They have said they will take us over," Rogers is quoted as saying. He urged the federal regulatory authority to accept "a new type of commitment to competition between the cable television industry and the telephone companies." The merger of Canadian Cablesystems and Premier Communications was seen by Rogers as enabling the cable TV industry to develop innovative services faster than the telephone companies.[10]

Competition between cable TV and telephone companies for this new market is occurring as fibre optics technology promises to free telephone companies from the limitations of conventional copper wire telephone lines. A single optical fibre, using light rather than electricity as its medium of transmission, can carry up to 4,000 voice conversations, hundreds of millions of "bits" of computer data, and up to six TV channels at the same time. This immense capacity would give telephone companies the ability to provide virtually all communications services to the home.

Bell-funded research on fibre optics between 1976 and 1980 amounted to about $18,600,000. Bell installed its first optical fibre underground in Montréal in October, 1977. Despite the higher cost of optical fibre — about 10 times the cost of paired copper wire — Bell Canada intends to install 100,000 kilometers of optical fibre telephone lines in this decade.

The most extensive use of optical fibre is planned in Saskatchewan where the publicly-owned telephone company, Saskatchewan Telecommunications, has announced a $56,000,000, four-year project to install a 3,200-kilometer optical fibre network across the province connecting communities of 500 or more households. This "electronic highway", according to SaskTel, is based on the premise that a telecommunications delivery system is a natural monopoly, that carriers of communications cannot interfere with content, and that "the ideal delivery system in a democracy...must give every person the equal right to communicate both as a sender and a receiver of messages."[11]

Telephone and cable TV companies and broadcasters may face videotex competition from other communications companies. CNCP Telecommunications, for instance, operates *Infoswitch*, a network for transmission of computer data, in competition with the Datapac service offered by telephone companies belonging to the Trans-Canada Telephone System. CNCP has requested permission from the CRTC to offer its customers a news database as an experiment. Trans-Canada Telephone System has filed an application with the CRTC to launch Canada's first computer messaging service — a form of electronic mail — using the public telephone network. These refinements of networks originally designed to transmit data between computers in commercial or government service would create delivery systems that could be used for carrying videotex services.

These services could be received on the screens of home computers as well as on the Telidon terminals being manufactured for the field trials. According to a recent analysis of import statistics, 55,000 microcomputers were imported into Canada in the year ending June, 1980. This analysis led to a forecast of 150,000 microcomputers to be imported in 1981, as costs declined. Between 1978 and 1979, average per unit import value dropped from $2,248 to $732. One major supplier estimated that 50 per cent of his 1980 microcomputer sales went to business, 40 per cent to education, and 10 per cent to hobbyists using small computers in their homes.[12] Estimates of the number of small computers that will be in Canadian homes by 1985 range from 10,000 to 50,000. Even at the slowest estimated rate of growth, the total of home computers in Canada in the next few years will dwarf the number of Telidon terminals manufactured for the videotex field trials and the first operational Telidon systems.

As in the United States, the growing number of home computers will shape the development of videotex in Canada. An initial example of integration of systems occurred in the spring of 1981 when a leading U.S. manufacturer of home computers, Apple Computer Inc., concluded an agreement with Infomart of Toronto to market an attachment for the Apple microcomputer that will enable it to function as a Telidon terminal.

The convergence of an "American" consumer market for home computers made in the United States and served mainly by U.S. databases, and videotex systems on the "European" model financed largely by government, would create in Canada a special challenge for policy-makers concerned about the orderly development of videotex. The growth of the home computer market, the proliferation of videotex trials, and the involvement of some of Canada's largest newspaper groups in these trials indicates that the time for creative policy formation may be short. Structures and business relationships already in place will dominate the initial development of Canadian videotex and, before too long, may be difficult to alter.

References

1. Tom Paskal, *Videotex Field Trials*. Research study for the Royal Commission on Newspapers, 1981. Public Archives. Subsequent information on Canadian field trials comes from this source unless otherwise noted.
2. Pierre Gaujard, "Videotex: Immediate Prospects". *Inside Videotex*, Infomart, 1980 p. 107.
3. Gordon B. Thompson, "Technology and the Information Society." *In Search*, Spring, 1980. p. 26.
4. Larry Wilson, "Bell Canada's Vista Project." *Inside Videotex*, p. 79.
5. Mike Aysan, "Project Ida: Home of the future." *Inside Videotex*, p. 66.
6. Canada. Department of Communications, News Release, November 6, 1980.
7. Canada. Department of Communications, News Release, January 28, 1981.
8. CRTC, Public Announcement, June 6, 1978.
9. John Howkins, "Canada's Communications Kaleidoscope", *Intermedia*. 8(6), November, 1980. p. 9.

10. "Rogers wants control of 1 m. TV sets." *Gazette*, Montréal, April 10, 1981.
11. Tom Howe, "Everyone-to-everyone." *Report*, September, 1980. p. 29.
12. Data Laboratories, *Analysis of the Impact of Electronic Systems on the Advertising Revenue of Daily Newspapers*. Unpublished report for the Institute for Research on Public Policy and the Royal Commission on Newspapers. Montréal, 1981. Public Archives.

8
Canadian newspapers and the information society

Not surprisingly, the growing concentration of newspaper ownership in Canada has been reflected in electronic publishing from the outset. Unlike some newspaper publishers in the United States and some European countries, where attempts have been made to stop or delay the introduction of videotex, Canada's largest newspaper concerns have invested heavily in the new technology. The two dominant groups in daily newspaper publishing, Southam Inc. and Thomson Newspapers Limited, are deeply involved in various forms of electronic publishing, as is the largest independently-owned newspaper, the Toronto *Star*.

Thomson is the owner of Info Globe, a division of the *Globe and Mail* of Toronto, the only Canadian newspaper that has transformed its archives into a computer database. Info Globe updates this information bank daily and markets it to customers outside its own organization. The Toronto *Star*, through its parent company, Torstar Corporation, is a partner with Southam in Infomart, a joint venture involved in virtually every aspect of electronic publishing. Infomart today is the giant of this infant industry, far more predominant in its own field than any single enterprise in the publishing of daily newspapers.

In no other country has a single commercial electronic publisher, specializing in preparing and marketing computer-stored data for videotex systems, achieved such a position. Through the assistance of government, and its own willingness to invest heavily in a speculative venture, Infomart has established a near-monopoly in the provision of services for the early development of videotex. Rivals may appear in the future, but its competitors at the moment are almost insignificant.

The origins of Infomart lie to some extent, paradoxically, in a regulatory attempt some years ago to encourage more competition in Canadian media.[1] When the CRTC in 1968 opposed cross-ownership of newspapers and broadcasting, the policy affected the future of Southam Press Ltd., as Southam Inc. was called before 1978. With a minority interest already in radio and TV stations through Selkirk Holdings Ltd., Southam was forced to explore other electronic avenues. In the early 1970s, under the direction of Michael Harrison, who had joined Southam in 1968 as vice-president, broadcasting, the company examined a wide array of highly experimental, and largely unmarketable, new technologies including video records and cassettes, educational and promotional video productions, computerized listing of apartment vacancies, and closed-circuit TV for apartment buildings. This strategy was based on the assumption by Southam, according to the recollections of some of those involved, that the company had to identify new "information manipulation-dissemination starting points" because "print orientations were going to become less and less the critical mass".

By 1972, Toronto Star Ltd. also was seaching for ways to lessen its almost total dependence on newspaper operations for revenue. Under the guidance of Roy Megarry, an accountant with experience in computers and management who joined the *Star* in 1974 as vice-president, corporate development, the *Star* investigated new information technologies so that its income would "not be as dependent on economic conditions as (is) the revenue from advertising dollars invested in the *Star* and the publications of our other companies".

The *Star*'s first foray into electronic publishing in 1974 wasn't promising. In an informal partnership with Maclean-Hunter Ltd., another print publisher interested at the time in computer-based information services, the *Star* developed a form of teletext transmitted on closed-circuit cable. The prototype was demonstrated informally for Pierre Juneau, then chairman of the CRTC, now deputy minister of communications in Ottawa, who reportedly had reservations about the technology as well as about the entry of two major news publishers into a new type of information distribution.

Talk of a joint venture in electronic publishing between the Toronto *Star* and Southam first came about through contacts between Michael Harrison and Roy Megarry. In 1965, the two companies had formed a joint venture, Southstar Publishers Ltd., to publish the weekend rotogravure supplement *The Canadian*. Megarry was invited to join Southstar's board and it was there, in 1974, that the decision was made to launch a joint venture in electronic publishing.

At about the same time, Harrison had hired Georg Mauerhoff, a computer librarian from the National Science Library, to design a major electronic publishing operation for Southam that would involve the creation of original Canadian databases. In 1975, this scheme was rejected, at least partly because Megarry felt that the Canadian market could not support it. After Harrison left Southam, Infomart was launched formally in October, 1975, as a Canadian sales agency for U.S. databases. Infomart continues to be active in this area, with about 500 database customers, but still no Canadian database of its own.

The announcement of Telidon in 1978 coincided with discussions about videotex among Torstar, Southam, and Bell Canada. Both Southam and Bell had been studying Prestel in Britain. According to one of the participants in these discussions, it was suggested informally at that time that Torstar, Southam, and Bell should form a joint venture that could dominate the development of videotex in Canada. Bell discouraged this, perhaps because of regulatory restrictions on its activities. In September, 1978, in the midst of these talks, Megarry left Torstar to become publisher of the *Globe and Mail*, then owned by FP Publications.

During the 1970s, the *Globe* had explored electronic publishing from a different angle. Under David Rhydwen, then its librarian, the newspaper had signed an agreement in 1975 with QL Systems of Kingston, Ontario, to develop a program to transform the *Globe*'s library into an electronic information bank. The decision to do this had been made in principle by the time Megarry was appointed publisher. Soon after his arrival at the *Globe*, Megarry persuaded FP Publications to commit $3,000,000 to Infomart. For a brief time, until FP Publications withdrew from the joint venture in September, 1979, Infomart involved three major newspaper groups — Torstar, Southam, and FP. There were hopes at that time that the *Globe* would provide the Canadian database that Infomart lacked.

After the withdrawal of FP from Infomart, on the advice of Megarry who by then had become skeptical about the potential consumer market for videotex, Info Globe was created in 1979 as a division of the *Globe and Mail*. Sale of the *Globe* to Thomson has had little effect on its operations. In Canada, Info Globe is Thomson's only electronic publishing activity, although the company is involved in videotex in the United Kingdom through its travel businesses. Info Globe's database now contains 250,000 items from the *Globe and Mail*, dating back to November 14, 1977, and updated every day. The staff of seven was servicing 370 clients in January, 1981, an increase of more than 200 compared with a year earlier. This included 35 clients in the United States. The number of clients is limited because of the high cost of the Texas Instruments terminal normally used to access Info Globe — about $2,500. The service continues to operate at a loss.

As it now stands, Info Globe's system is not compatible with Telidon. Its database will not be accessible to Telidon terminals until computer programs are created to "translate" existing North American databases into Telidon's distinctive computer language. This is technically feasible, according to Telidon's designers, but little research is under way in this area.

One of Megarry's final contributions to Infomart, before leaving for the *Globe*, was the hiring of David Carlisle as president. Carlisle, formerly with IBM Canada, had been vice-president, marketing and technical, at Datacrown, the Toronto data processing company that provides services to Info Globe. Under Carlisle, the company has expanded dramatically. Since the autumn of 1979, Torstar and Southam have shared equally in a total investment of $12 million. The number of people employed at Infomart has increased from 12 to more than 150 as of June, 1981. Its corporate divisions reflect Infomart's range of activities: technical services, marketing, operations, videotex services, and database publishing.

Database marketing is the company's original activity. There now are more than 500 users of Infomart's U.S. databases. A Canadian business information database, B&G News, was abandoned in 1980 after losing more than $300,000. Infomart's total database business in 1980 was estimated at more than $700,000 but that sector of the company was still operating at a loss.

About three-quarters of the Infomart budget is devoted to videotex development. Revenue from videotex in 1980 was less than $400,000. Infomart's projections of revenue for 1981 ranged up to almost $7 million.

Stimulated by government investment in Telidon, Infomart's videotex activities have expanded rapidly. Videotex services, launched in 1979 under Martin Lane, a veteran of the Prestel system, employed four designers and eight writers in January, 1981, with most of the writers recruited from copywriting departments of advertising agencies. In 1980, Lane's division created 5,000 videotex pages for such clients as Project Ida and Grassroots in Manitoba, Bell Canada's Vista in Québec and Ontario, and Canadian Cablesystems' franchises in Portland, Oregon, and Erie, Pennsylvania. Lane expected to create more than 20,000 pages in 1981, still a relatively small number in relation to the 100,000 pages that Vista proclaimed as its objective in 1981.

Marketing activities are directed by several key executives who worked with Carlisle at Datacrown. Recruitment from the computer industry has strengthened Infomart's sense of its own identity as a "computer utility", to use Carlisle's description, rather than as a publishing subsidiary of Torstar and Southam.

Infomart's vice-president of technical services, Fritz Gaffen, is also from Datacrown. Gaffen is writing the computer programs that will enable the Telidon system to be used for an electronic ombudsman service in Venezuela, a telebanking system in Canada, or any of the other applications that the marketing branch believes it can sell. In 1980, Infomart spent more than $1 million developing this software; in 1981, the total was likely to be almost $1,500,000.

Infomart's revenues are increasing largely because of contracts for Telidon systems. Among the most important are:

- Teleglobe Canada. A $1,100,00 contract for a turnkey or ready-to-use system to transmit a Canadian business information database internationally. Teleglobe will employ about 50 user terminals initially.
- Times-Mirror Company. A $1,000,000 contract with the Times-Mirror Company of Los Angeles for a turnkey Telidon system for a trial in Southern California.
- Venezuela. A $1,000,000 contract, shared with a Venezuelan subsidiary, for a Telidon turnkey system to display government information in public places in Caracas.

Infomart also is playing a major role in providing computer, page preparation, and information services to Bell Canada's Vista trial of Telidon in Ontario and Québec, to the three Telidon trials using facilities of the Manitoba Telephone System, and to Rogers Cablesystems for its U.S. franchises. Although telephone and cable TV companies are competitors for future videotex markets, Infomart at the moment supplies both.

Despite its success in obtaining foreign contracts for Telidon against competition from British and French systems, Infomart remains a highly speculative venture. In mid-1980, Torstar reported six-month profits almost 15 per cent lower than in the previous year. The decline was attributed to investment in Infomart, as well as other factors. The chairman of Torstar, Beland Honderich, has said that Infomart profits in the short term will depend on contracts from business and government. In the long run, he has stated, the "consumer home mass market holds by far the greatest profit potential, but it will probably be five to 10 years before it makes a significant profit contribution."[2]

If videotex fails to develop as an important mass communication medium, newspaper groups involved in Infomart and, to a much lesser extent, Info Globe, will have weakened their basic industry to no purpose by shifting investment away from newspapers. If videotex succeeds, they may be in a position to establish a degree of dominance at the outset that it took some Canadian newspaper groups more than a century to achieve in print.

References

1. Ian Brown and Robert Collison, *Newspapers and Videotex*. Research study for the Royal Commission on Newspapers, 1981. Public Archives. Subsequent information on Infomart and Info Globe comes from this source unless otherwise noted.
2. Edward Clifford, "Torstar Will Try to Offset Effect of Rates". Toronto *Globe and Mail*, April 17, 1980, p. B6.

9
The future of videotex

Trying to forecast the future of videotex, and its effect on newspapers and other media, is the original videotex industry and, so far, the most profitable one. Consultants have made careers out of it and academics have thrived on it. Little of their activity is of much help to the politicians, bureaucrats, and businessmen who now find themselves dealing with the initial effects of what may be a tidal movement in communications.

The difficulties of forecasting, admittedly, are awesome. To understand the complex technology is to risk losing sight of its potential to alter human behavior in many respects. To be overwhelmed by visions of its potential as an agent of change, as were many of the original prophets of the "wired community", is to lose sight of myriad practical difficulties. To concentrate on the expense and time required to build new systems, which is the current fashion in forecasting, is to overlook the human appetite for progress and the breathtaking ability of new information systems to bring human society to a new level of self-knowledge and capability.

Despite all this, various attempts to forecast have not been entirely wasted. Impressions have been gained from the welter of conflicting estimates to produce a "feel" about the future, if not hard forecasts. The feeling now is unmistakable. Something important appears to be in progress, even if it remains impossible to say how, where, and when it will manifest itself.

In almost every country, the introduction of videotex has been accompanied by exaggerated forecasts of future developments. This happened in Britain, where Prestel and its information providers still are trying to recover from the non-appearance of the predicted residential market. Early in 1979, the British Post Office was estimating that there would be 100,000 Prestel subscribers by the end of 1980. The actual total was less than one-tenth of that.

A study of the Canadian market in 1979 estimated that there would be 40,000 Telidon subscribers by the end of 1981. At the beginning of 1981, there were fewer than 400 Telidon terminals in use and no "subscribers" at all in the commercial sense. The same study projected 200,000 subscribers in 1984 and 620,000 in 1986.[1]

More realistic was a U.S. study in 1978 that included a summary of negative factors affecting the growth of videotex: uncertainty about privacy and security of electronic systems, legislative and regulatory confusion, and lack of computer and communications software. "The net effect of the various factors is somewhat negative now," concluded this study, "but will swing to positive by 1982 and will be practically compelling by 1988."[2] This 1978 forecast has stood the test of time better than most. It is generally assumed now that the moment of decision for videotex as a mass medium will arrive some time between now and 1985. If the decision is for continued development, the impact of videotex will be significant toward the end of the decade and in the early 1990s.

A major study by the Boston consulting firm of Arthur D. Little in 1979 for a group of American and Canadian publishers concluded that videotex would not offer significant competition to newspapers before the end of the decade, but that the future of newspapers was uncertain after 1990.

In Britain, forecasters of videotex development with working experience have tended to be more conservative than the communications theorists. The marketing manager of the "world's first electronic newspaper" in Birmingham, for instance, stated that it will be four or five years before the residential market for Prestel starts to grow significantly, and 10 to 12 years before Prestel creates something that might be described as a mass audience.[3]

Guided by initial estimates of the Canadian market done for the Department of Communications, the minister of communications in 1979 stated that there was "reason to believe that the number of Telidon subscribers could exceed 600,000 by 1986."[4] David Carlisle, the president of Infomart, has made a recent, more detailed prediction leading to the same conclusion: 5,000 Telidon terminals by the end of 1981; 25,000 by the end of 1982; 75,000 by the end of 1983; and 500,000 by the end of 1984.[5] In announcing additional funding for Telidon in February, 1981, Communications Minister Francis Fox predicted that more than 12,000 Telidon terminals would be in use within a year.[6] This number of terminals, if achieved, would comprise only a test market. The minimum number of terminals for a successful commercial videotex market in Canada has been estimated at 50,000.[7]

The most recent and comprehensive attempt to estimate the impact of videotex on Canadian newspaper advertising, prepared in 1980-81 for the Institute for Research on Public Policy by Data Laboratories of Montréal, contained a "fast development scenario" that envisaged 225,000 videotex or microcomputer terminals available in Canada by 1985 to access Telidon systems. About 60,000 of these would be in homes. This would not be a significant advertising market but achieving this "could establish the framework for a greatly expanded consumer home use of videotex in the late 1980s and 1990s". The study warned newspapers that videotex could change advertising patterns "quickly and discontinuously" in the late 1980s. Stating that the growth of a new advertising medium can occur only at the expense of existing media, the study concluded that newspapers will be most affected by the growth of advertising on videotex, and that radio and television networks will be most vulnerable to competition from pay-TV and prerecorded video material.

As Gordon Thompson wrote in the spring of 1980, even if videotex trials are reasonably successful in the next few years, and the first operational systems are built, there is still "the last peril, where the system lives, but only with enough vigor to be barely discernible...".[8]

Even in the fastest videotex scenarios, newspapers still have at least a few years to brace for the onslaught. Perhaps they have decades. Regardless of the timetable, the threat to newspapers clearly is there and, perhaps, more lethal in its potential than the impact of radio and television has been.

References

1. John Madden, *Videotex in Canada*, Department of Communications. p. 28.
2. Tim Tyler, *Electronic versus Paper Media*, San Jose, Calif.: SBS Publishing, May, 1978, p. II-4.
3. Interview with John Foxton, Birmingham, February, 1981.
4. Canada, Department of Communications, News Release, April 2, 1979, p. 4.
5. Ian Brown and Robert Collison, *Newspapers and Videotex*. Research study for the Royal Commission on Newspapers, 1981. Public Archive.
6. Canada. Department of Communications, News Release, February 6, 1981, p. 3.
7. Brown and Collison, Research study.
8. Gordon B. Thompson, "Technology and the Information Society," *In Search*, Spring, 1980. p. 26.

10
Protecting the individual

The existence of many newspapers in a single community used to provide a competitive market for the services of journalists, who enjoyed the freedom of craftsmen to sell their talents to the highest bidder. This freedom was never absolute in practice, but it helped to protect the independence of journalists.

The growth of monopoly newspapers has been accompanied by the rise of unions to protect the independence and the livelihood of journalists. One of their recent concerns has been the role and status of journalists in new information systems. This has been expressed, in practical terms, in negotiations over the rights of journalists to benefit from "replays" of their work on videotex. In the United Kingdom, the question of "intellectual property" has been raised by the National Union of Journalists; in the United States, it has been a basic issue in negotiations between The Newspaper Guild and newspapers in at least two cities.

In Minneapolis, in a 1980 strike at the *Star* and the *Tribune*, newspapermen proclaimed common cause with members of the Screen Actors' Guild who were on strike at the time for royalties on films and television series replayed on cable television or sold on videocassettes or videodiscs. "Just as actors wanted payment for their performances when 'resold' on videodiscs," wrote Michael Anthony, the music critic of the *Tribune*, "striking reporters demanded compensation if their work wound up on computer screens around the country."[1]

The question surfaced in Minneapolis because the *Star* and *Tribune* were among newspapers which had entered into an agreement with CompuServe, the data-processing company, to have all their news processed and sold to CompuServe subscribers for a six-month trial period. CompuServe had announced plans to make news from 14 newspapers and the Associated Press available to 5,200 owners of home computers by the middle of 1981. "There is a growing awareness among reporters," wrote Michael Anthony, "that electronic news could turn into an enormous moneymaker in years hence. A lot of us don't fully understand the potential of it, but the feeling among reporters is we better get it right away, because once the thing starts to roll, it may be too late."[2]

In Minneapolis, the Guild contract had contained a provision entitling union members to 25 per cent of net profits, or a minimum fee of $75, from the resale of their work to print media. The company, in the 1980 negotiations, wanted to eliminate that clause. In a compromise settlement, the company agreed to retain it but refused to extend it to include electronic media. The company explained its position by saying that the $75 minimum fee would have applied every day to every reporter whose work appeared on videotex. This would have made it too expensive for the Minneapolis newspapers to participate in the CompuServe trial, according to Stephen Isaacs, editor of the *Star*.[3]

At the Chicago *Sun-Times*, the contract for years had contained a standard clause guaranteeing that "any employee whose work is sold after publication in the *Sun-Times* shall be given additional compensation... amounting to no less than 50 per cent of the proceeds." The Guild met with more success there than in Minneapolis. The contract was settled 45 minutes before the strike deadline when the *Sun-Times* agreed to retain the clause without changes.

"The *Sun-Times* caved in," Isaacs of the Minneapolis *Star* was quoted as saying, "and they're probably not going to participate in the CompuServe experiment because of it. What may eventually happen with papers that can't get the clause dropped, or at least get a waiver for electronic news, is that they may just refuse to pay and let the Guild fight it legally. Labor lawyers have told me it's a very close call."[4]

At issue here is more than the compensation of journalists or the ability of newspapers to evolve into suppliers of news for videotex. The quality of the information on the new systems is the ultimate consideration. The videotex industry, at least in its present form, does not originate news. It is not involved in journalism; its business is the processing or "reformatting" of news for videotex, storing it in a computer, and transmitting it to viewers on request. Journalists may process the news, as in the United Kingdom, but this also can be done by copywriters trained in advertising agencies, as in Infomart in Toronto.

Before news can be processed for videotex, a journalist has to gather information, assess it, structure it, and write it. By far the largest number of journalists who are doing this today are still working for newspapers and other print media. Much of the so-called "electronic journalism" on radio and television depends on the print media as its primary source of information. As we have become more adept at processing and distributing news, this journalistic base has deteriorated. In many communities, with monopoly daily newspapers, fewer print journalists are covering fewer aspects of society for fewer readers than in previous years when there were many competitive newspapers. If this process of technological advance and editorial deterioration continues, the new media will suffer at the outset from all the problems of contemporary print journalism and will make no contribution to its improvement. A way will have to be found, as videotex develops and perhaps threatens even monopoly newspapers, to invigorate the journalistic base, where news is first received and formulated, with revenues from the new means of processing and distributing news. This is in the long-term interest of newspaper proprietors as well as journalists. If negotiation fails to achieve this, copyright laws may have to be reviewed to ensure that journalists share in the benefit gained from new uses of their intellectual property.

Many other legal questions are raised by the spread of computer communications and the development of videotex. Questions about ownership relate not only to copyright but to responsibility for the electronic publication of material. If one has been libelled on videotex, for instance, and the libellous material has been erased from the computer's memory within seconds of its transmission, how is proof of publication to be obtained? Up to now, questions of this type have been the subject of academic rather than courtroom discussion. The experience of Prestel indicates that they may be more daunting in prospect than in reality.

Questions related to privacy are more immediate. They have existed since the start of computer communications. If videotex becomes widespread, invasion of privacy may seem more imminent to more people. Even the test systems contain features which, in the interests of efficiency, infringe on concerns that always have been private.

Concern about privacy and computers has been, up to now, of more interest to policy-makers than to the average citizen. In 1972, a survey for the Department of Communications indicated that more Canadians were worried about the effects of computers on employment than on personal privacy. Seventy-one per cent agreed that computers cause unemployment, but only 37 per cent agreed that they threaten to invade privacy.[5]

The 1972 report of a federal task force on "Privacy and Computers", established by the Departments of Communications and Justice, recommended standards for computer security and legislation to ensure privacy. No federal legislation dealing specifically with privacy and computers has resulted from this but Manitoba, Québec, Ontario, and Saskatchewan have enacted privacy statutes, following the 1968 example of British Columbia.[6] The 1977 Canadian Human Rights Act does contain the legislative framework for the protection of personal information under the control of the federal government. The Act provides for the appointment of a Privacy Commission with investigative powers and enables the government to make regulations in the field of information processing, storage, and transfer within federal jurisdiction.

Despite the proliferation of official studies of computers and privacy, Canada lags behind some European countries in taking a comprehensive and focused legislative approach. The Data Protection Act in Germany, for instance, calls for the establishment of a "Data Protection Commissioner" on the federal level, functioning both as an "ombudsman" and as a national advisor on data protection matters. The same Act calls for the establishment of State Supervisory Boards by the Lander and the appointment of Data Protection Officers in private corporations.

The problem and the potential solution were summarized in 1976 by Douglas Parkhill, assistant deputy minister in the Department of Communications. Describing the threat to privacy, Parkhill said: "The various data files — medical, educational, financial, legal, law enforcement — as they become interconnected, could make available in a conveniently accessible form a complete record of the most intimate information about everyone, including malicious gossip and rumors." On the other hand, "this same computerization provides us with an opportunity to employ protective mechanisms far more effective and rapid in their response than are feasible in a manual system."[7]

As videotex systems move from the laboratory to field trials, questions of privacy become real. Even at this early stage, they complicate such an apparently simple matter as billing for videotex services. Traditionally, only one's news vendor knew which newspaper one bought and, by inference, something about one's tastes in politics and other matters. Coin-operated vending machines eliminated even this friendly surveillance. Videotex systems in which the user pays the information provider for information, and billing is done by some central agency such as the telephone company, contain horrendous possibilities for misuse of information about our personal lives. If we are what we eat, as it is now fashionable to say, we also are what we read. Commercial advertisers are interested in the former, but the latter conceivably could be of compelling interest to the state. Bernard Ostry, then deputy minister of communications in Ottawa, warned in 1979 that "one can imagine an unscrupulous carrier giving this information to credit companies, the police, political enemies, employers, private security companies, or even local gossips." Ostry also indicated that the problem might contain its own solution. Carriers of videotex will have to ensure privacy, he suggested, otherwise "most people will probably refuse to buy two-way TV if they begin to suspect it's some sort of omniscient cathode eye eavesdropping in every intimate nook and cranny of their lives."[8]

In actual practice, in Britain, this has not been a problem. The British Post Office does all the billing for Prestel, charging the customer for telephone service and information provided, and forwarding money to the provider. It can and does collect information about total usage of different pages in its information bank, but carefully avoids recording data that would show types of information accessed by individual subscribers. The French are convinced that billing by a central agency is prohibitively expensive. They are experimenting with a magnetic videotex "charge card" that users would insert in a "reader" attached to a videotex terminal. Every use of the terminal for a certain length of time would subtract, invisibly and indelibly, a portion of the videotex "credit" recorded on the card. When the credit is used up, a new card would be issued. If practical, this system would ensure as much privacy for the consumer of news as the coin-operated newspaper vendor.

Videotex trials in Canada do not involve charging for information, but in the Vista trial, for instance, the telephone company will log data about usage of various pages in the information bank. This recording of types of content flowing within the system will be a new role for Bell and one that may need scrutiny in view of the legislation that requires Bell to "act solely as a common carrier".

Infringement of privacy, if it occurs, may be cloaked in the guise of improved service to the consumer. An early example of this, already present in Canadian field trials, is "telemetering" of water or energy consumption in the home. An interactive system provides the capability of remote metering and billing for services other than videotex, television, and telephone usage. Utilities providing water, electricity, or gas can take advantage of this. When the "telemetering" circuit is two-way, the next step is "telecontrol" of consumption. J.W. Fraser, Bell Canada's assistant vice-president of business development, reported in 1980 that several Canadian telephone companies are "actively involved in defining and dimensioning this service".

"From the utilities viewpoint," he said, "the benefits may include reduced costs for meter reading, the ability to remotely transfer power loads, identify and isolate faults, and restore service, as well as the ability to control power loads during peak periods. For the residential customer, it would result in a new rate schedule based on usage by time of day. All of these capabilities add up to a more efficient use of energy and we believe that, over the next decade, that's a real contribution."[9]

The ability to "telecontrol" has been built into Project Ida by the Manitoba Telephone System but deliberately not tested. According to MTS Product Development Manager Mike Aysan, this company is "hoping we can go to the other, better alternatives where we'll give financial incentives to shift toll peaks into our valleys...telemetering can support that just as telecontrol can support the Attila the Hun punishment solution. If you don't know how far this horror has gone, and you would like to see an application of this nature," Aysan told a 1980 videotex conference in Toronto, "Pacific Tel and Power Authority in California are currently under way with such a system. It's operational, and the regulatory body expects that within 24 months eight per cent of all Californians will be on such a system."[10]

Harking back to the freedoms enjoyed by journalists and their readers in the ancient world of competitive newspapers shouldn't tempt us to think that newspapers by definition are a more liberating medium than newer channels of journalism. Recent changes in the economics of newspaper publishing have made print journalism a more confining profession. The introduction of computers now leads newspapers to dream of imitating some of the marketing efficiencies of electronic media. Several of Canada's largest newspapers already use computers containing circulation data to control automatic bundling and labelling of newspapers as they come from the press. Improving this technology would enable newspapers to allocate a particular copy of the newspaper to a particular reader. Automatic sorting machines eventually will have the ability to assemble, for every reader, a custom-made newspaper containing only the sections requested by the reader. Those preferences, listed and classified by the computer, would give newspapers a new marketing instrument to compete with the ability of videotex to discriminate between users. If and when newspapers achieve this, differences between newspapers and videotex, as far as individual privacy is concerned, may not seem as important as they do now. Legal devices to ensure privacy and individual freedom may have to apply to both.

References

1. Quoted in Richard Reeves, "Who Owns Videotex?" *Panorama*, February, 1981. p. 8.
2. Ibid.
3. Ibid., p. 9.
4. Ibid.
5. Cited in "The Social Implications Information Processing," by H.H. Brune, Computer/Communications Secretariat, University of Waterloo, 1978. p. 9.
6. Charles Dalfen, Regulatory aspects of the New Technology. Research study. Public Archives.
7. Douglas Parkhill, "Who's Afraid of Computer Communications?" *In Search*, Autumn, 1976. p. 10.
8. Bernard Ostry, "The Two-Way TV Revolution." *Perception*, November/December, 1979. p. 26.
9. J.W. Fraser, Paper presented to the Canadian Telecommunications Carriers' Association, Vancouver, June 23, 1980, p. 13.
10. Mike Aysan, "Project Ida." *Inside Videotex*. Infomart, 1980. p. 65.

11
Protecting the nation

In the information society, the flow of information is as vital as the supply of food. National information systems must be potentially self-sufficient and secure if a country values its independence. Some day this consideration may be irrelevant. If the information society creates a new order of interdependent nations, the free flow of information will bind together the human community. Even in that new order, however, individuals and communities may want to build fences to shelter their native cultures. For now, past experience dictates the principles that are applied to the flow of information across national borders. It is a question that has concerned many countries.

Since 1975, more than 35 European nations as well as Third World countries have enacted or are considering data protection laws to restrict the flow of personal records and other data across national borders. Over the past two years, the Organization for Economic Co-operation and Development has prepared guidelines on the protection of privacy and trans-border flows of data that have been adopted by 18 of the OECD's 24 member governments. They state that trans-border data flows should be "uninterrupted and secure."

The question of trans-border data flows has occupied Canadians since the first computers arrived from the United States. There has been concern, broadly speaking, about the economic and cultural effects of an open border, but the potential loss of business has seemed to be more worrisome than possible threats to national sovereignty.

"The principal problem," according to the 1972 Report of the Task Force on Privacy and Computers, "is not one of the privacy of Canadian data subjects being invaded by data about them stored in the United States. It is rather that data processing and communications business may be lost to Canadians as a result of this foreign flow; that data in United States data banks might be pre-emptorily withheld abroad for a variety of reasons, including security regulations, court injunctions, etc.; that United States laws might change and leave Canadians less well protected; and that, as a sovereign state, Canada feels some national embarrassment and resentment over increasing quantities of often sensitive data about Canadians being stored in a foreign country."[1]

Subsequent studies have attempted to estimate the threatened loss of business. An interministerial group in Ottawa published a report in 1978 showing that imports of computer services have gradually increased since 1973. They grew to an estimated value of $155,000,000 in 1975, which represented about 30 per cent of the services obtained by Canadian users from other than in-house sources. If the trend continues, imports of these services will reach $1.5 billion by 1985 and account for about 52 per cent of the Canadian market.[2] According to the 1978 Ottawa study, Canada will not be able to offset this by increasing exports.

It was reported in 1978 that 7,500 workers in the United States were employed in serving Canadian data processing needs. This is expected to increase to about 23,000 by 1985.

The danger for Canada was described succinctly by a U.S. communications expert in 1979: "While most of the U.S.-based jobs will be in systems and programming, computer operation and management activities," wrote Oswald H. Ganley, of the Program on Information Resources Policy at Harvard University, "Canadian officials say the lower paid data conversion staff and some data control staff will form the greater part of the jobs remaining in Canada. In fact, the deepest concern of Canadian officials and other groups is that with the export of data processing activities from Canada to the U.S.A., top management will also move steadily to the U.S.A., and that decisions will thus be made increasingly in U.S. corporate headquarters rather than in Canada. Canadian middle and upper management may become superfluous, since they will have nothing left to manage. This state of affairs is considered potentially disastrous to the growth of the economy and the nation."[3]

This concern in Ottawa is not reflected within Canada's computer industry, which has sought more freedom and less interference by government. Two or three of the largest Canadian companies export from 10 to 20 per cent of their services to the United States; servicing U.S. clients brings Canadian companies more than $10,000,000 worth of processing business every year. The Canadian companies want Ottawa to help them to expand this business by reducing taxes and tariffs, not to impose restrictions on trans-border flow which raise the possibility of similar action by Washington.

"Information flow is not something you can control by geographic boundaries," according to Gerry Meinzer, the head of the Canadian Association of Data Processing Organizations.[4]

Partly because of this opposition, the Canadian government has been slow to act. There are some 23 items of federal legislation relating to where information may be stored and 92 provincial laws and regulations that may be relevant but enforcement has been feeble. They have had a negligible effect on the flow of data between the two countries. One exception to this is the new Bank Act, passed in 1980, which requires Canadian banks to do their data processing in this country. If the government follows recommendation of the 1978 Clyne Committee on the Implications of Telecommunications for Canadian Sovereignty, it will consider extending this requirement to such other industries as insurance and loan companies.

Legislation has been promised to permit Statistics Canada to measure the outward flow of data. The Department of Communications has assembled an interdepartmental task force which is expected to make policy recommendations on transborder data flow in 1982.

The flow of computer data across the Canadian-American border has been measured, up to now, primarily in terms of dollars and jobs. The cultural threat has been more difficult to define. In 1978, the Science Council of Canada stated that "a new technology has begun to affect the lives of Canadians. It seems inevitable that we will, at some point, have some form of public interactive communications/information service. We must ensure that we adopt the system that is optimal for our needs and not one that has evolved without planning and been put together in a patchwork fashion."[5]

A new study by the Department of Communications, entitled The Information Revolution and its Implications for Canada, warns that the revolution "may accelerate the erosion of national sovereignty by further increasing the dominance of multinational corporations."[6] Describing the havoc that natural disasters or massive social or economic disruptions might wreak on computer installations that have become essential to society, the report also warns that "Canada may be more vulnerable than many other countries" to these disruptions "given the relative size of Canada to the United States, the particularly high level of U.S. investments in this country and the increasing flow of data across the border".[7] Canada would have no protection from disruptions that might have nothing to do with conditions inside Canada.

The "optimal system" cited by the Science Council in 1978 still seems remote. Discovering it will seem more urgent as videotex takes computer data out of the office and into the home. If videotex becomes a news and information medium akin to broadcasting in its reach and influence, undoubtedly there will be demands to bring videotex under broadcasting legislation to ensure that it is effectively owned and controlled by Canadians so as to "safeguard, enrich and strengthen the cultural, political, social and economic fabric of Canada".[8]

At the moment, Canadians who own computer terminals enjoy unrestricted access to databanks in the United States. Telidon videotex terminals now being manufactured are not able to access U.S. databanks, because of Telidon's distinctive computer language. This technical barrier will not long remain if Telidon becomes an American standard or if computer programs are devised to make different systems compatible.

There is every reason to believe that videotex technology will tend to increase the international flow of news and information, particularly between countries with the same language and similar cultures. This is, indeed, one of the objectives of Teleglobe Canada, the Crown corporation which is in the process of organizing a Telidon service specifically to supply Canadian information to clients in other countries.

Canadians believe in the freest possible flow of information. It would be difficult for any Canadian government to restrict Canadians' access to databases anywhere in the world, even if it were feasible to do so. At the same time, the principle of free access to databases in other countries must not be applied at the expense of Canadian capacity to gather, assess, and distribute information about ourselves to ourselves. These systems form, in a sense, a representation of national memory and national consciousness. The arguments that have protected Canadian newspapers, periodicals, and radio and TV stations from foreign ownership apply with even more force to videotex systems.

Because of market conditions and, more recently, government policy, foreign ownership of newspapers has not been an issue in Canada, as it has in the United

Kingdom. Even the recent newspaper closings have prompted only a few, hesitant suggestions that this field should be opened to foreign investors, as a desperate measure to restore competitive conditions. Because of the vulnerability of Canada to U.S. influence, Canadians have seen no contradiction in restricting ownership of newspapers and other communications industries in Canada, while applauding Canadian entrepreneurs who expand into newspaper and other communications ventures in the United States and other countries. The same rationale justifies ensuring that videotex databases serving the general public should be majority-owned and controlled by Canadians. This could be accomplished by regulatory restrictions on ownership or by tax regulations affecting Canadian dollars spent on advertising and other commercial videotex services.

The free flow of information across our borders would continue to give all Canadians access to information anywhere in the world; Canadian databases also would be able to import and market data from other countries. It may remain more economical and convenient for Canadians to access databases in Canada, when the information is available here, rather than going to more distant sources outside the country. Revenue from imported databases could help pay for the creation of Canadian databases.

The initial experience of Infomart and Info Globe has shown that the creation of commercial Canadian databases is almost prohibitively expensive, even for our largest media conglomerates. It should be government policy to encourage the creation of commercial databases as an essential research and development activity.

The role of videotex as a national medium of news and information, delivered primarily by telephone line and coaxial cable, and perhaps later by optical fibre, may be critical if satellite communications make a bureaucratic shambles of attempts to protect national radio and television systems from international competition. Even as the CRTC attempts to assess the economic and social implications of direct-to-home satellite transmission of radio and TV programs, rooftop receivers are becoming almost as popular in some parts of Canada as were backyard stills during periods when sales of liquor were prohibited.

Ensuring that videotex systems form an integral part of our national media system, and accurately express our national identity, means helping to provide Québec society with the ability to use the new technology. Fears have been expressed in France about the effects of a technology that uses English not only as the primary international language for the storage of information but as the language most often used by programmers who design systems to employ computer hardware for specific tasks. The French have perceived telematics as a threat to the culture and languages of countries where the new technology is received passively, relying on imported equipment and ideas. This fear has motivated France's attempt to promote the development of videotex systems constructed by and for its own people.

This concern applies even more forcefully to the smaller French-speaking society in Canada.

Québec itself has been slow to appreciate the implications of videotex and slower still to take part in its development. It was almost as an afterthought that Québec was included with Ontario in the Vista trial by Bell Canada, the telephone monopoly that serves both Québec and Ontario. Although newspapers such as *Le Soleil* and *La Presse* have shown interest in videotex, and the videotex project of

Télécable Vidéotron in the Montréal region is one of the most ambitious proposals in the country, there are no counterparts in Québec to Infomart or Info Globe. The development of an electronics industry in the Ottawa Valley, encouraged by the Department of Communications, has taken place mainly on the Ontario side of the Ottawa River. To a certain extent, Telidon has remained an English-speaking technology, devised and manufactured by English-speaking Canadians.

In Québec, there has been an undercurrent of academic concern for some time. In 1976, Robert Talbot, an adviser at Québec's Université Laval, warned that "no vehicle of our culture is so precious as language — yet during the next 20 years, no other cultural determinant will feel the effects of computer communications more strongly. The language of computers is English," he wrote. "Most of the developments, both in hardware and software, have taken place in the United States, and an adequate knowledge of English is needed to access the large data banks. Without it, there is a real danger of being cut off from the main information systems. This is a risk French-speaking people in Canada cannot afford to take.

"But what can we do?" he asked. "It would cost far too much to set up special French-language data banks for Québec. Simultaneous translation, which is technically feasible, would be an even worse solution because it would subject the character of the French language, its syntax and semantics, to too great a strain. So far as language is concerned, computer communications has rubbed salt in an already open wound. In many fields today — scientific, technical, and intellectual — French-speaking people are cut off from prime sources of information by their poor command of the English language. Quebecers face the challenge of protecting their language without depriving themselves of the very real benefits of computer communications."[9]

Québec society has moved slowly to confront this awesome difficulty, despite the Québec government's concern about jurisdiction over established forms of electronic communications. Recently, there have been a few signs that the federal government's interest in Telidon since 1978 has been noticed in Québec. An article in *Le Devoir* in November, 1980, dealing with Telidon as part of a short treatise on "les télécommunications, enjeu politique" (telecommunications, the political stakes), warned that "Québec should not keep out of this new field of jurisdiction". The writer continued: "Ottawa seems to have understood the political stakes involved in telecommunications and is well out in front in making sure it has the controlling hand....Computerization is a development which not only increases productivity and thus improves our competitive position on the world market, but also alters traditional power relations to the benefit of whoever controls access to information. Under the Canadian system of governmental powers, that means reinforcing the central authority to the detriment of the provincial, which will have to accept federal authority."[10]

It should be taken for granted, in any discussion of videotex development in Canada, that governments in Ottawa and Québec will make the special efforts that will be required to create French-language databases and to develop the expertise of Quebecers in other aspects of the videotex industry.

The Commission's research has shown the dangers of a simplistic approach to this question. As one of our studies suggested, "one doesn't have to believe that culture is threatened because the large cultural institutions are tottering on their foundations." The study distinguishes between various groups within society, each of which uses and affects information media in its own way: "When one claims that national cultures and linguistic communities are threatened by the standardizing influence of videotex, one confuses communities of interest and culture communities; one reduces the role of language which is both a vehicle for communication and a receptacle of cultural values."[11] Support for videotex research and development in Québec and among French-speaking communities outside Québec should encourage the development of new approaches to information technology within these groups without imposing criteria from the English-speaking community.

References

1. Cited by Oswald H. Ganley in "Communications and Information Resources in Canada." *Telecommunications Policy*, December, 1979. p. 271-272.
2. Ibid.
3. Ibid., p. 273.
4. Kari Sweetman, "Data 'tide' is flowing out of Canada," Ottawa *Citizen*, February 23, 1981.
5. Science Council of Canada, *Communications and Computers*. Ottawa, 1978. p. 37.
6. Shirley Serafini and Michel Andrieu, *The Information Revolution and its Implications for Canada*. Ottawa, Department of Communications, 1980. p. 28.
7. Ibid., p. 29.
8. Broadcasting Act, R.S.C. 1970, c.B-11, s. 3.
9. Robert Talbot, "New Threat to an Embattled Culture?". *In Search*, Winter, 1976, p. 20-21.
10. "Les télécommunications, enjeu politique." *Le Devoir*, November 21, 1980.
11. Jean-Paul Lafrance, *Nouvelles techniques et concentration de la presse au Québec* (*New Technology and Ownership Concentration in Québec*). Research study for the Royal Commission on Newspapers, 1981. Public Archives.

12
Freedom of the electronic press

Questions of privacy, copyright, and trans-border flows of information have existed from the beginning of the computer age. They inspired a considerable body of theoretical knowledge and state regulation long before the first videotex systems came into being. These systems pose new regulatory questions, arising from the electronic transmission of information in print, an apparent merging of print and broadcast media.

In North America, publishers of newspapers, and radio and television broadcasters, belong to different communications eras with distinctive technologies and relations to the state. Newspaper publishers in recent times, as a rule, have been businessmen antagonistic to interference by the government. The state has not licensed or regulated newspapers in Canada, the United States, or Britain. By contrast, from the outset, the state has allocated the limited number of radio and television frequencies to state and private enterprises, and regulated broadcasters' performance. In Canada and Britain, the role of the state in broadcasting has been more varied and influential than in the United States.

Videotex can merge print and broadcast media. In doing so, it transmits the product of the unregulated newspaper industry through a regulated medium. Newspaper publishers claim the tradition of a free press must be protected regardless of the means of delivery. Broadcasters, on the other hand, demand that a new competitor in their medium operate under the same regulations as they do. In some countries, newspaper publishers have attempted to use regulatory agencies to stop videotex services by broadcasters or telephone utilities. This tactic has been used in the United States against American Telephone and Telegraph, and the outcome of this dispute could influence regulatory decisions in Canada.

Technical advances and regulatory decisions in recent years have opened new avenues of activity to AT&T. Many of them are beyond the company's original mandate to carry telephone messages. Some infringe on the role of the printed press as a conveyor of news, information, and advertising.

For some time, AT&T, and telephone companies in other countries, have been supplying "news" or information of various kinds to their subscribers. The most common is recorded time and weather announcements, but other information that can be obtained from telephone companies in different parts of the world covers such categories as tourism, motoring, recipes, sports results and schedules, gardening, racing, and exchange rates. In New York, in 1979, the seven counties around Manhattan generated 271,000,000 announcement service calls producing a reported revenue of $16,000,000. In the words of John C. LeGates, director of Harvard University's Program on Information Resources Policy, AT&T could use these services to "get its nose under the tent of information services generally, and begin to condition people to use the telephone when they want to know something."[1]

At the same time as AT&T has been exploring the use of the telephone system to provide information, regulatory decisions have weakened barriers that once prevented it from expanding into new activities. In a 1956 consent decree settling a Justice Department suit that sought to break up AT&T, the company agreed to limit its activities to telecommunications and to stay out of data processing. Since then, however, the two fields have become almost indistinguishable, melding into one vast information business. As a result, the 1956 decree effectively was set aside in 1980 by the final decision of the Federal Communication Commissions's Second Computer Inquiry which abandoned as unworkable the distinction between communications and data processing services. New regulations permit a "dominant carrier" such as AT&T to supply new services provided they do this through "arms-length subsidiaries".

The general tendency to deregulate private industry in the United States has fostered the liberation of AT&T from earlier restrictions, despite fears that this development will mean less rather than more competition, in this case, as AT&T is freed to forage widely in areas served by its smaller competitors. AT&T already has announced preliminary steps to create what its prospective competitors in the computer industry have called "Baby Bell". By any standard other than the size of the parent company, this baby will be a giant. One financial analyst in New York has estimated that the new subsidiary could grow into a $10 billion business by 1985, selling equipment as well as electronic directory and data processing services.

The "arms-length" provisions are designed to prevent AT&T from cross-subsidizing its unregulated data processing business with money and proprietary information from its basic telephone service, which remains a regulated monopoly. Even if this separation is effective, "Baby Bell" in its infancy could be the second-largest computer firm in the world, after International Business Machines Corporation.

Newspapers were among the industries alarmed by AT&T's entry into fields that they had considered their own. Although U.S. newspaper publishers favored deregulation in principle, they have opposed its consequences in the case of AT&T, arguing that AT&T's size and monopoly power in regulated markets would make it an unfair competitor in the business of providing information. The American Newspaper Publishers Association also stated that AT&T should not be allowed to provide information over its own communications system in competition with other providers using the same system.

In Texas, a recent attempt by Southwestern Bell Telephone Company, an AT&T subsidiary, to launch a computerized news and information service on a trial basis has been opposed, in what may be a significant test case, by The Texas Daily Newspaper Association. "They not only want to transmit the information," said

John Murphy, executive director of the newspaper association, "they want to be the gatherer and the provider."[2]

The newspapers' opposition to AT&T was flawed, to some extent, by the rush of some U.S. newspapers to invest in cable TV systems and to participate as information providers in videotex trials. In Miami, for instance, the Knight-Ridder newspaper group, one of the largest in the United States, is conducting a videotex trial in partnership with AT&T as it bids for a cable TV franchise in another part of the country.

Because there was no Canadian equivalent of the 1956 consent decree in the United States that prevented AT&T from engaging in data processing and other unregulated activities, several smaller Canadian telephone companies and CNCP Telecommunications were offering data processing services in the late 1960s. The carriers' right to do this in competition with unregulated companies offering the same services was defined in the 1972 Report of the Canadian Computer Communications Task Force, which suggested that separate affiliates be created by the carriers for this type of business. In a 1973 statement, the federal government approved the "entry of the federally-regulated communications carriers into the computer services industry...through the mechanism of a separate arms-length affiliate."[3] The device of an arms-length subsidiary was included in a set of guidelines issued in 1975 by the federal ministers of finance and communication but it has never had legal force.

As a result, telephone company practice in this field has varied. Member companies of the Trans-Canada Telephone System offer data processing services through its Computer Communications Group, not a subsidiary of the telephone companies but part of the TCTS partnership. In 1980, Bell Canada established a wholly-owned subsidiary, *Intelterm*, to sell "intelligent" data communication terminals. Bell also has an electronic publishing subsidiary, Teledirect, to publish "yellow pages" on videotex and to provide videotex services to other information providers.

In the United States, the recent AT&T decision to create "Baby Bell" has raised questions among newspapers and computer companies about the effective divisions between parent companies and their arms-length subsidiaries. As Harvard's John C. LeGates told directors of the American Newspaper Publishers Association in 1980, "different lengths-of-arm may be specified between the subsidiary and the parent". LeGates referred to "the myth of separate subsidiaries" in cases where both parent and subsidiary companies use the same plant or, in AT&T's case, the same communications networks.[4]

Perhaps the lack of landmark regulatory decisions in Canada and the gradual involvement of communications carriers in computer services is responsible for the relatively slow response of Canadian newspaper publishers to the same situation that has alarmed many of their U.S. counterparts. The participation of some of Canada's largest newspaper groups in videotex services provided by telephone companies also may be a factor. Whatever the reasons, there has been little outspoken support among Canadian publishers for the kind of position taken before the Royal Commission in February, 1981, by Walter J. Blackburn, publisher of the London *Free Press*, an independent daily newspaper. Blackburn stated that Bell Canada and the Trans-Canada Telephone System are "the greatest single threat to daily newspapers in the future, due to their immense wealth, extensive wire network, and the Canadian satellites in which they have a substantial interest". He saw the entry of Bell and other telephone companies into electronic "yellow pages" not only as a threat to newspaper advertising revenues but as the first step toward a larger information role. "From there, with their part in content established," he said, "the world is theirs."[5]

Newspapers' objections to competition by telephone companies are based on more than the fear of new commercial competition. Two principles are involved: freedom of the press, and the separation of carrier and content. The first originated in the age of print; the second belongs to the electronic era.

In Western society, freedom of the press is based on the right to publish information without prior consent of the state, and more recently on the citizens' right to information. Applying these principles has created in the past a numerous and diverse press, which, with all its excesses, is still the most direct way, according to democratic experience, of reaching the truth. In his 1859 essay *On Liberty*, John Stuart Mill wrote that "only by collision of adverse opinions" can the truth be ascertained and maintained. This remains an article of faith, even among the publishers of today's monopoly newspapers.

Chief Justice Lyman Duff, in the Alberta Press Case of 1938, after noting that "freedom of discussion of public affairs means...'freedom governed by law,'" insisted that "it is axiomatic that the practice of this right of free public discussion of public affairs, nothwithstanding its incidental mischief, is the breath of life for parliamentary institutions."[6]

Freedom of the press, in the words of a 1945 U.S. Supreme Court decision, "rests on the assumption that the widest possible dissemination of information from diverse and antagonistic sources is essential to the welfare of the public, (and) that a free press is the condition of a free society."[7]

The same arguments used by some newspapers to oppose competition in news provision by telephone monopolies have been applied, in Canada, to the participation of a few newspaper groups in the videotex industry. This involvement was a source of concern to many who appeared before the Commission.

According to the brief submitted by the Canadian Labor Congress, the people who own and direct the newspaper conglomerates are on their way to controlling the new electronic information systems. Referring to newspaper involvement in videotex trials in North America, the CLC brief stated that this issue was being raised "not to sound a conspiratorial tone, or to forecast the ultimate demise of the traditional newspaper, but rather to raise before this Royal Commission the spectre of the newspaper industry reaching out into new technological territory".

"Who will own these new systems?" asked MP and former journalist Pat Carney at the Commission's hearings in Vancouver. "Are we all going to end up working for Southam News Service or Ted Rogers of Canadian Cablesystems?" [8]

Also in Vancouver, the Commission was warned by David Godfrey, chairman of the department of creative writing at the University of Victoria and co-author of *Gutenberg Two*, that "if there is not to be a similar Commission 30 years down the road, struck into being by the merger of Imperial-Torstar-Maclean-CP with Thomson-Brascan-Irving-Dominion... then it might be instructive to look now at theoretical remedies, however fantastic, because those theoretical remedies can be applied in advance to the new media.

"And the way I look at those remedies," Godfrey continued, "is by asking the simple question: how in the boardrooms of the nation will they, are they planning now, to manipulate the new media? How can one manipulate the new technologies so that concentration is possible, profitable gateways are seized, entry thresholds to new competitors are raised, and profits are insured, all without incurring government intervention?"[9]

On the other side of this question, Infomart, with the support of the Department of Communications, has drawn attention to the risk involved in videotex investment and its potential to provide a competitive marketplace for various types of information providers. "We don't see any huge central databases, as I believe you heard about in Vancouver," the Commission was told in Toronto by David Carlisle, president and chief executive officer of Infomart. "We see a proliferation of many small and very inexpensive databases."[10]

After informing the Commission in Ottawa of details of the relationship between Infomart and DOC, the department's assistant deputy minister, Douglas Parkhill, asked: "Does it give their owners (the owners of Infomart) some sort of privileged position? In the sense that they are gaining early experience through their subsidiary in the operation of a Telidon system, the answer is yes." He went on: "But I would also ask, what is wrong with that? The same could be true of any other information providers in this country. It just so happens that before anybody else, those particular newspapers, newspaper chains, recognized the importance of this and invested very heavily in it. . . . So I don't really think that the fact that these two newspapers have been receiving — at least, that a subsidiary of theirs which is performing an extremely valuable national service — I don't really detect any menace here, although obviously it is important that when it comes to fostering the generation of information, that the government spread its money around. And we certainly intend to do this."[11]

At issue here, and in the debate over the role of telephone companies in videotex, is the question of accessibility to the new medium. Who will be able to publish on it? Whose voices will be heard?

In our own time, the number and variety of newspapers have been affected by competition from electronic media and other factors. They may be further reduced if videotex systems become important carriers of news, information, and advertising. If the carrier systems operate news services themselves, in competition with other information providers, the result could be monopoly news services provided by telephone and cable TV systems that are licensed and regulated by the state. In such a system, freedom of the press, as defined for centuries, would be extinguished almost by accident, through the unifying effects of modern technology and corporate management.

Anthony Smith, the author of *Goodbye Gutenberg*, believes that the ideals and traditions of the printed press will help society, as it passes through the age of electronics, "to find ways to re-establish and reguarantee the basic individual freedoms of expression and of information".[12] Among the first of the new principles to become firmly established is the separation of carrier and content. No such distinction was required in the old world of competitive newspapers where as many "channels" of print communication existed as there were publishers with enough time, money, and talent to realize their ambitions. It becomes necessary in a world of vast systems of communication enjoying monopolies in their own territories.

This separation is easily stated and achieved in the telephone system. Bell Canada is expressly prohibited by law from controlling or influencing the messages that are the content of its carrier system. As the systems proliferate in number, type, and purpose, the distinction becomes harder to define and maintain.

Except in the case of telephone companies, the federal government has an attitude rather than a policy on content/carrier separation. It was described to the Commission by Parkhill as "a new fundamental dichotomy: a total separation of carrier and content, of the distribution systems and of the services that they distribute".[13]

Parkhill was repeating for the Commission ideas he had been developing within the Department of Communications for some time. In 1980, he had stated, "We are saying — as the way that Canadian policy is developing — that there should be a wall of separation between those who distribute the information, the monopolies that everybody depends upon, and those who have to make use of their carriage facilities."[14]

"What we have here," Parkhill had written in 1979 in *Gutenberg Two*, "is recognition that in terms of regulation, the marriage of computers and communications leads us logically to a new fundamental dichotomy: a total separation of Container and Content, of the Electronic Highways and of the services that they distribute."

Parkhill listed three elements common to most definitions of carrier-content separation:

- A total ban on any carrier involvement with content.
- An obligation on the part of the carrier to meet any reasonable demands for service.
- A legal requirement on the part of the carrier to distribute the services of all suppliers on a non-discriminatory basis at authorized tariffs.[15]

Recent experience indicates that maintaining this "wall of separation" in videotex may be difficult. In Britain, the informal screening of information providers, allotment of computer space, and control of Prestel indexes by the British Post Office reveals a substantial degree of content control by the carrier.

Similar breaches of the wall are evident already in Canadian videotex trials, particularly in the publishing of electronic "yellow pages" by subsidiaries of telephone companies and in the companies' control of computer information banks and the indexes that guide users to their various sections.

In 1980, Larry Wilson, director of business development for Bell Canada, stated, "We do not intend being in the content-provisioning area." Then he went on to qualify this statement of intention by saying:

> Referring to the yellow pages, we already have moved into that with an arms-length subsidiary named Teledirect. They intend on being an active information service provider. Having said that, it is a bit of a grey area. In the front end of the videotex system, there is an indexing function, and there are instructions as to what's new on Vista. That's content of sorts. Second, there is also storage of information provided by others (non-Bell) which can be retrieved by videotex users.

> The first area, or indexing of information on the system, is fairly clear to us as a legitimate role for us. It is directly associated with the telecommunications function. The second area we see as gray. There are some in government and in our own company who are a little unsure about just what the proper rights are in that area, but we think it's such an important requirement of the system that we are treating computer storage as a telecommunications function and, therefore, we will be doing that.
>
> As far as the actual content goes, we will not be providing it, and again one must separate field trials from all the statements I have made earlier. For a field trial, we think we can bend the rules a bit, and if some of the contents that we would like to see on the system don't appear, we may well insert them ourselves, as we did the mortgage calculation capability in the pilot system.[16]

Watching these services develop, some authorities already have seen the need to strengthen "Parkhill's wall". David Godfrey asked the Commission to "clarify the split once and for all".

"No carrier ought to be able to provide any content whatsoever," he said. "I would go further than Parkhill and remove even the traditional directories from the economic domain of the carrier."

Godfrey suggested that there should be an "intermediary body between the carriers and information providers...that should have something of the status of notaries or lawyers dealing in trust".[17]

The publication of "yellow pages" directory advertising on videotex by telephone companies may be regarded as provision of content by a carrier, in competition with other providers.

Indeed, describing this type of videotex advertising as "yellow pages" is misleading. Directory services now published by telephone companies are limited in their usefulness because of space restrictions and publishing schedules. Videotex advertising will provide almost unlimited space and can be updated continually. Because of their inherent limitations, printed telephone directories do not compete with newspapers in a substantial way. "Yellow pages" on videotex, however, could be a new and highly competitive advertising medium.

Since the motivation for videotex publishing of this type by telephone companies is commercial, the relevant questions are: is the best use of new revenues from videotex advertising to subsidize other services of the telephone companies? Or should the telephone companies confine themselves primarily to their original business of providing carrier services to all private and commercial clients on an equitable basis? Proponents of carrier/content separation argue that, because of the inherent conflict of interest, telephone companies should produce videotex directories containing only the names, addresses, and numbers of telephone or videotex subscribers, grouped, in the case of companies, according to services or goods offered. Newspapers and other information providers should be free to compete for videotex advertising. A new field of activity for telephone companies may be the publishing of printed directories of videotex services.

So vital is the separation of carrier and content to the development of a diversified, competitive, and free electronic press that governments should err on the side of caution when carriers seek to expand into activities related to content. Allowing

"Parkhill's wall" to be undermined during videotex trials may prevent it from ever being firmly established.

Any discussion of regulation of videotex in Canada occurs against a background of federal-provincial dispute over jurisdiction. Broadcasting is most apparently a federal concern, and has been regulated as such, but federal jurisdiction over cable TV has been disputed. Provincial authorities regulate eight of the 10 largest telephone companies.

According to a recent study of communications policy by the Howe Institute,[18] full-scale federal-provincial conflict began in 1973 when Ottawa tabled its proposals for a national communications policy. Québec led the opposition to Ottawa's initiative by demanding virtually complete control over communications policy. All the provinces joined in a statement to Ottawa in 1975 supporting "increased provincial decision-making" in communications. The provinces argued specifically for jurisdiction over "all aspects of cable distribution systems and services with the exception of federal broadcast services".

According to the Howe Institute study, the federal-provincial conflict over communications policy that raged in the 1970s entered a period of "uneasy quiet" at the start of the new decade, "but it is not yet clear whether this portends some broader peace or is merely a lull before the next storm". The Institute forecast that provinces "undoubtedly will become increasingly important in communications policy-making".

Although it is common to blame federal-provincial wrangling for delays in implementing a comprehensive communications policy, Canada is not the only country beset by regulatory squabbles and probably not the worst afflicted. Several U.S. commentators recently have analysed Canada's "unique mixture of monopoly, competition, regulation, and co-operation in industry structure and government oversight" [19] and one of them, Harvard University's Oswald H. Ganley, stated that "this system has served Canada well.... Canada has demonstrated possibly the lowest degree of regulatory lag of any western industrial democracy".[20] Within the context of this continuing debate over federal and provincial jurisdiction, guidelines for the development of various videotex systems can be discussed on the assumption that freedom of the press is the main objective, and that separation of carrier and content contributes to this.

A. Broadcast teletext

Teletext, a form of videotex transmitted in the vertical blanking intervals of conventional television channels, can complement and enhance television programming with additional print information. Revenue from this type of service would seem to belong properly to the broadcaster rather than to an information provider licensed in competition with the broadcaster.

Allocating this new medium to the broadcaster, rather than to print media, would back up the Canadian Radio-television and Telecommunications Commission's policy of encouraging diversified media ownership.

In both Canada and the United States, regulations have discouraged cross-ownership of print and electronic media, although each country has adopted a different approach. In the U.S., the Federal Communications Commission (FCC) limits by regulation the number of radio, television, and daily newspaper enterprises held by a single owner, but there are numerous exceptions to the rule. In Canada, the CRTC has rejected an approach based on numbers of enterprises owned in favor of case-by-case determinations.

The principle guiding CRTC decisions that involve ownership concentration was stated in a 1978 ruling: "To the extent that concentration of ownership and control in the Canadian broadcasting system increases...diversity of opinion and information available to Canadians is potentially reduced."[21]

In regard to broadcasting-newspaper cross-ownership, the CRTC stated in 1979 that:

> The ownership and control of broadcasting undertakings should be separate from the ownership and control of newspapers except in special circumstances. The Commission has been particularly concerned with the level of cross-ownership of broadcasting and daily newspapers in view of the potential reduction in independent and separate editorial judgments that this could involve. This would be of greater concern if there was joint ownership of broadcasting and newspapers in the same market.[22]

The trend toward homogenized information would be even more pronounced in a community where broadcast teletext further integrated television and newspaper news operations under the same owner. This possibility should strengthen the arguments used by the CRTC in its efforts to see that Canadian communities have media that accurately express their diversity.

B. Cable teletext

Cable TV was originally no more than a carrier of television programs aired by broadcasters and received on a community antenna. Cable companies were assigned exclusive territories and have been regulated, since 1968, by the CRTC. The industry since then has become a hybrid, involved not only in the distribution of broadcasts but also in the production and transmission of new programs and services. Videotex presents new opportunities for both aspects of these operations.

Cross-ownership between telephone companies and cable systems has been prohibited. Cross-ownership between television stations and cable systems has existed for many years, though not as an arrangement favored by public policy. Again, diversity of ownership has been the objective. In numerous decisions over the past two decades, the CRTC has expressed its opinion that, "except in special circumstances, television undertakings should be independent of cable television undertakings...."[23]

Until 1978, cable systems in Canada were not permitted to offer other services, apart from community programming. In that year, the CRTC announced that it did not intend to "inhibit...the development of innovative services by the Canadian cable television industry". It stated that it would give "prompt and favorable consideration to applications by cable television licensees for the use of their systems to provide new communication services of a non-programming nature".[24] Videotex and teletext are services that cable TV companies now want to offer in response to this invitation.

The largest such company, Rogers Cablesystems, told the Commission that in the United States, "not only are all new cable television plants built completely two-way, but the regulatory environment is such that cable operators are encouraged to provide a proliferation of services". (In fact, they are required only to have two-way capacity through later adaptation of equipment.) In Canada, according to Rogers, "neither telephone companies nor the cable companies are encouraged to seek roles as deliverers of in-home information services".

Again, according to Rogers, separation of carrier and content, which it described as an "old telecommunications-based notion", no longer serves as a framework for guiding the development of new information technologies. Rogers has stated that it "no more believes that cable operators should be denied access to their own system than should broadcasters, newspapers or any other information providers be denied access to the cable system".[25]

This position, in effect, claims for cable TV as a hybrid system all the advantages that belong to both broadcasters and communications carriers without any of the restrictions. The cable TV industry asserts that this dual role, as both carrier and provider of information, would be compatible with a policy assuring other information providers equal access to cable systems.

If this were granted, there would be no reason to restrict the activities of telephone companies as information providers. Conversely, if telephone companies are permitted to provide content through arm's-length subsidiaries, it is hard to argue that cable systems should not have the same right.

Removing the wall of separation between content and carrier in this fashion would favor the development of monopoly information services on videotex with no significant benefit except to cable systems and telephone companies which already are large, monopolistic by nature, and profitable. It would seem more in line with current public policy to encourage cable systems to market their carrier services among new information providers, at least until there is evidence that competitive videotex and teletext services cannot be developed without the direct participation of cable systems.

C. Videotex by cable

The reasons for restricting cable systems to being carriers of teletext, even if the teletext is a new service using the vertical blanking interval of a channel already used by a cable operator for community or other programming, apply even more forcibly when two-way videotex services are transmitted by cable.

In the interests of competition with as little state regulation as possible, providers of these new services should be able to compete within the "marketplace" of a cable system whose primary concern is transmitting the services as efficiently and as profitably as possible. The main regulatory function, in this case, would be to ensure equality of access to all potential information providers and the allocation of channels to non-profit community activities.

D. Videotex by telephone

The introduction of videotex holds out the promise of greater utilization of telephone systems and increased revenues for telephone companies operating in their traditional role as carriers of information. Unless it is shown that the competitive free enterprise system cannot provide the new services made possible by videotex technology, telephone companies should concentrate on their role as carriers only, leaving provision of content to others.

* * *

The test of new information systems is their contribution to freedom of the press as it has come to be understood in our society. There should be the widest possible access to publishing in all media, with a minimum of supervision by the state.

As communications and information systems develop, this accessibility may be easier to achieve when consumers are provided with multi-channel home information systems. Up to now, the state has acted as allocator of a limited number of electronic channels. All the regulatory apparatus of radio, television, and telecommunications has originated from that function. This foundation will crumble as communications and computer technology creates an almost infinite number of channels, bringing within our reach a freedom to publish undreamed of even in the golden age of competitive print journalism. In principle, the new technology should make access to electronic publishing cheaper, easier, and less restricted than is newspaper publishing today, perhaps unencumbered by the regulatory apparatus that radio and television have had to bear.

References

1. John C. LeGates, "Changes in the Information Industries", speech to the Board of Directors of the American Newspaper Publishers Association, September 11, 1980. p. 3.
2. "U.S. Newspapers Seek to Block Bell's Information System." Montréal *Gazette*, December 23, 1980.
3. Hon. Gérard Pelletier, Minister of Communications, "Computer/Communications Policy: a Position Statement by the Government of Canada." April, 1973.
4. LeGates, "Changes in the Information Industries", p. 9.
5. Royal Commission on Newspapers, *Transcript of Proceedings*. p. 1897-98.
6. Reference re Alberta Statutes (1938) 2 S.C.R. 100.
7. Statement by Justice Black in the U.S. Supreme Court decision in United States vs. Associated Press. 326 U.S. I (1945).
8. *Transcript*, p. 1725.
9. Ibid., p. 1745-46.
10. Ibid., p. 2305.
11. Ibid., p. 6475-78.
12. Anthony Smith, *Goodbye Gutenberg*. Oxford University Press, 1980. p. 299.
13. Douglas F. Parkhill. Brief to the Royal Commission on Newspapers, 1981.
14. *Inside Videotex*. Proceedings of a seminar, March, 1980, Toronto. Infomart, 1980. p. 16.
15. David Godfrey and Douglas Parkhill, eds. *Gutenberg Two*. Toronto. Press Porcépic Ltd. 1980. p. 82.
16. *Inside Videotex*, p. 80.

17. David Godfrey. Brief to the Royal Commission on Newspapers, 1981.
18. Brian Woodrow *et al*, *Conflict over Communications Policy*; Montréal. C.D. Howe Institute, 1980.
19. Oswald H. Ganley, "Communications and Information Resources in Canada." *Telecommunications Policy*. December, 1979. p. 280.
20. Ibid.
21. CRTC, Decision 78-669, October 12, 1978. References to CRTC documents are cited in Charles Dalfen, *Regulatory Aspects of the New Technology*. Research study for the Royal Commission on Newspapers, 1981.
22. CRTC, Notice of Public Hearing, February 9, 1979.
23. CRTC, Decision 74-58, March 26, 1974.
24. CRTC, Public Announcement, June 6, 1978.
25. Colin D. Watson. Brief to the Royal Commission on Newspapers.

13
Concentration of ownership

Despite the theoretical possibility of "every man becoming his own publisher" on videotex, the Canadian videotex industry at this early stage shows a tendency to concentration which is related to newspaper concentration but may also be encouraged by the nature of the technology in its current state of development.

Advances in communications technology present this paradox: the promise of expressing the diversity of mankind, and the reality of vast and costly networks operated by state and commercial corporations that regard mankind as little more than a mass audience. These networks are designed to cover audiences as thinly and as widely as possible rather than to explore the deep resources that exist within every human being and within the smallest human community.

The invention of writing is said to have destroyed the closeness and continuity of cultures that depended on the spoken word. Written records were a source of power for the first civil and religious bureaucracies. The invention of printing coincided with the development of modern national states and international empires. Within the world of newspapers, advances in computer and communications technology have encouraged publishing operations of unprecedented scale. Following examples in other countries, using the latest technology, the *Globe and Mail* of Toronto in 1980 became in reality what it had long proclaimed itself to be — English-speaking Canada's first national newspaper. Satellite communications enabled the Globe to use printing plants in Québec and Alberta, later in the Maritimes and British Columbia, to publish newspapers that reached subscribers across the country as rapidly as those in Toronto. Pride in this recent achievement still obscures the danger that it may pose for local newspapers, particularly if the Globe exploits its new potential to create distinctive editorial packages for regional audiences, supported by regional advertising. Local newspapers owned by the proprietor of the national newspaper may find themselves becoming local supplements of the national edition, having lost in the process the capacity to interpret national and international events for their own communities.

In television, satellite communications now are threatening the national networks that seemed, only yesterday, so large and invulnerable compared with newspaper operations. Canada is among many nations struggling to develop satellite systems to beam television programs to small "backyard" receivers and, at the same time, to prevent citizens from using this new capability to receive programs from the satellites of other nations.

In its earliest stages, videotex reveals the same tendency to encourage large-scale development by government and industry, despite all the original hopes that this would be the maverick technology that would protect and enhance individualism.

Optimism about videotex originated in the belief that it would bring information to people rather than people to information, that it would decentralize societies physically and intellectually. Once videotex networks were established, according to these utopian scenarios, the costs of using them would be relatively low. A whole range of new publishers or information providers would come into being. As David Godfrey speculated in *Gutenberg Two*: "Fotheringham will not need *Maclean's* to reach his audience, nor will Pierre Berton need Jack McClelland. But advertisers may need them both when the *Sun* and the *Province* fold and new avenues to consumers are required. By the time the *Sun* does fold, the smart reporters will have already picked their area of specialization and alone, or in small groups, or in co-operatives, or by going to work for Starbell on salary or contract or royalty basis, will have become information providers. If consumer groups, or women's groups, or Ford-owner groups, or religious groups don't like what's happening, they will be able to establish their own information group and become publishers — with an initial investment of less than $10,000."[1]

This promise of a "new individualism" is fading even as the embryonic structures of the videotex industry in Canada take shape. Videotex activity in Canada already is more highly concentrated than newspaper publishing, largely as a consequence of the domination of newspaper publishing by a small number of large groups.

The infant industry is dominated by one corporation of relatively gigantic stature, Infomart.[2] This domination has been fostered by government authorities who ostensibly have tried to avoid the kind of concentration that now exists. Despite a growing awareness of what has occurred, and apprehension about the corporate baby that is being nurtured on the placenta of state support for videotex development, it already may be difficult to change course. The pattern of future development may be inherent in the structures that are now in place.

At one point, early in its brief history, Infomart was owned by three of the largest newspaper groups in the country, Torstar, Southam and FP, and had fleeting dreams of adding Bell Canada to its progenitors. After Bell demurred and FP disappeared into the Thomson group, Torstar and Southam continued to operate Infomart as equal partners. Important as Torstar and Southam are in the world of newspapers and other forms of print and electronic communication, their share of conventional markets is insignificant compared with Infomart's domination of videotex activities in Canada.

Infomart's only significant competitor as an electronic publisher at the moment is Teledirect, the arm's-length electronic publishing subsidiary of Bell Canada. Compared with these operations, other electronic publishers are cottage industries. Infomart earnings were expected to reach $6,000,000 in 1981, with the largest share coming from government contracts for turnkey systems and videotex publishing services. Infomart's dominance is both the cause and effect of its close collaboration with the federal Department of Communications. Ottawa's decision in 1978 to promote Telidon aggressively marked a turning-point in Infomart's development. Before that, its business was primarily the marketing of U.S. databases in Canada. Expanding on this experience, Infomart was soon in a position to provide the database creation and market promotion services that Telidon required. At the outset, because of the financial resources of its owners and their management expertise, only Infomart seemed able to provide these services on the scale required. The federal government quickly became Infomart's most important client. As Infomart grew, it became more and more difficult for potential competitors to match its resources and experience.

The domination of Infomart has been achieved in collaboration with a government department dedicated, as its senior officials have stated, to achieving something quite different. Within a few months of Telidon's announcement in 1978, Douglas Parkhill of the Department of Communications publicly discussed efforts to bring together parties interested in its development: federal and provincial governments, manufacturers, information suppliers, and telephone and cable TV companies. Parkhill was quoted as saying that the technology ideally should be introduced by a "consortium of companies such as in the Canadian aerospace industry".[3]

The notion of a consortium had been included in a 1978 consultant's report by Hickling-Johnston Ltd. for DOC on strategy for Telidon field trials. Commenting on this in the spring of 1979, John Madden, who was then DOC's director general of Special Research Programs, referred to it as an "information consortium".

"Telidon vitally needs information providers of all kinds," he told a Toronto seminar, "and though I am highly gratified by the response we have had thus far, led by Torstar-Southam and *La Presse*, I am concerned about organization on the information provider side.

"What I suspect is needed is a central information distribution agency operating as a commercial enterprise and acting as a middle man for a welter of information providers of various shapes and sizes on the one hand and a smaller but nonetheless significant number of Telidon service deliverers on the other."

As a potentially major supplier of information and services itself, Infomart is not the "middle man" envisaged by Madden, although it can provide services of this type to smaller competitors.

"If this doesn't occur," continued Madden, "it may be that those with the most at stake in ensuring the success of Telidon (such as those delivering the service and possibly those manufacturing the equipment), would be prepared to invest in an information consortium specifically created for the purpose of being such a middleman."[4]

The Hickling-Johnston report had suggested that no single participant be allowed to hold more than 25 per cent of the equity. Madden agreed with this, suggesting that the consortium not only might package information for sale to Telidon service providers but also might market Telidon systems in other countries.

"Should such an organization come about," concluded Madden, "it should be clear from the outset that it would not be intended or indeed be permitted that it exercise monopoly control."[5]

Infomart now provides all of the services listed by Madden, and more. As a provider of information and creator of databases for other information providers, it dominates the new industry. As an international sales agent for Telidon, it has what amounts to an exclusive franchise at the moment. In an effort to avoid the kind of "ad hoc" relationship that now exists between Infomart and Telidon, the Science Council of Canada's Committee on Communications and Computers suggested a scenario in July, 1979, for the development of videotex.[6] The first steps of the scenario, Telidon field trials and the creation of a consultative committee to guide the Department, have been implemented. The subsequent steps recommended by the Council are:

- Publication of a position paper by DOC to propose specific regulatory policies on the provision of Telidon services and the technical standards of Telidon systems.
- Creation of a technical advisory committee to work on specifications and standards for operation.
- Public hearings on videotex.
- Introduction of a policy paper.
- Political consideration of policy and, finally, legislation.

These steps still provide a framework for orderly policy development but the Science Council's 1979 scenario is rapidly being overtaken by events. Infomart may soon reach the point where its dependence on the government will be less than the government's dependence on it. The heavy involvement of the Department of Communications in videotex depends on Telidon for its justification but Infomart's future may be independent of Telidon. As one Torstar executive has been quoted as saying, unofficially, "We're not committed to Telidon per se."[7] Infomart may well dominate videotex publishing in Canada regardless of the system that eventually is adopted, largely because of the funding made available to the Department of Communications for the promotion of Telidon.

The relationship between DOC and Infomart has flourished outside any framework of policy, despite fears of this type of concentration that were expressed at the outset of the development of Telidon at the highest level in DOC. It has flourished for obvious reasons, not because of any hidden conspiracy. DOC needed an organization such as Infomart to bring Telidon from the laboratory to the marketplace. Infomart needed help from DOC, in addition to investment by its owners, to go into business on a large scale before the marketplace for videotex came into being. Without Telidon, there would have been no rapid development of the videotex industry in Canada in the past few years, and nothing on the scale of Infomart today. There might have been, in its place, a much smaller industry dominated by foreign systems and information providers.

Despite the logic of the DOC-Infomart relationship, Infomart will be healthier in the long run if it can exist on its merits within a competitive industry rather than primarily on government contracts. DOC will be more comfortable when it can forget about the promotion and marketing of Telidon and return to its proper role of overseeing, among its other responsibilities, the orderly development of communications systems in Canada. The relationship between DOC and Infomart needs to be assessed with a view to diversifying the videotex industry and encouraging competition not only in the manufacture of hardware but in the provision of videotex publishing services and the marketing of videotex systems. This assessment is now under way within the federal government. Among the options being studied are several suggested by the Clyne Committee on Telecommunications and Canada: a joint venture involving government and the private sector for the development of Telidon, or the designation of "chosen instruments" for its manufacture and commercial exploitation.

"Unless Canadian governments and entrepreneurs step quickly into the Canadian vacuum," warned the Clyne Committee, in 1979, "it will soon be filled with foreign information products, and the opportunity for Canadian entry into the market will be lost."

The vacuum now has been replaced by a jumble urgently in need of rearranging before its temporary structures, some of them alarming, become permanent institutions.

References

1. David Godfrey, *et al. Gutenberg Two*, Press Porcépic, 1980. p. 5.
2. Information about Infomart in this chapter is drawn largely from Ian Brown and Robert Collison, *Newspapers and Videotex*. Research study for the Royal Commission on Newspapers, 1981. Public Archives.
3. Allan Bailey, "Videotex - the time has come." *Canadian Electronics Engineering*. October, 1978. p. 51.
4. John C. Madden, *Videotex in Canada*. Discussion paper prepared for Delta Dialogue Series Seminar, Toronto, May 8, 1979. Project Delta, Gamma/Université de Montréal/McGill University.
5. Ibid.
6. Science Council of Canada, *A Scenario for the Implementation of Interactive Computer-Communications Systems in the Home*. Ottawa. July, 1979.
7. Brown and Collison, Research study.

14
Information, knowledge, newspapers, and new ideas

To recapitulate: the activities in Canada described in this book are aspects of the development of an "information society". It is said that developed countries now are progressing from an industrial society to a society where information becomes the primary resource and generator of wealth. This perception has encouraged analysis of the nature of information and the imagined character of the information society.

As Innis and others have stated, information is not knowledge. The accumulation of information does not create wisdom. One of the fears of those who contemplate the prospect of an information society is that individuals and communities will be overwhelmed by an "overload" of information that could paralyze thought and prevent effective action. There is also concern that society might try to cope with this by entrusting the accumulation and classification of information to willing bureaucracies, state or corporate. This could lead to greater social and economic divisions and less freedom for the individual.

Perhaps there is a model of this type of society in the newspaper world today. Technology has enabled newspapers to process larger and larger amounts of information. As newspapers have fallen into the hands of computer experts and marketers of information, the quality of the information has tended to deteriorate. Originality of thought and craftsmanship in the writing and presentation of information have become less important than the techniques of moving larger and larger amounts of data quickly and profitably toward mass audiences. As the newspaper industry has become more efficient at doing this, newspapers have lost important segments of their audience and have experienced uncertainty about their real purpose. Information bureaucracies have flourished while there has been a decline in the freedom of the journalist to market his talent and the freedom of individuals to choose among a large number of competitive and affordable newspapers.

Newspapers have progressed as pipelines for information — or "information utilities" to use a contemporary description — while they have declined as interpreters of their times. The best newspapers historically have represented more than collections of data; they have provided a way of looking at the world, often one man's way. A newspaper is a cultural undertaking as well as a business enterprise. Like a theatre company or an orchestra, it requires the leadership of a dominant personality and it must express a recognizable and distinctive viewpoint to be successful. Newspapers published by large corporations with diverse interests have lost this character and, by their nature, can never attain it.

Large daily newspapers have become the dinosaurs of the media, impressive and vulnerable. The largest often are the least secure, requiring continual increases in advertising revenue to satisfy their voracious appetites for newsprint and to subsidize their expensive distribution systems. Even relatively small changes in the economic context in which they exist, or interruptions of normal publishing schedules because of internal problems, can be enough to topple these giants.

In our own time, the last of the daily newspapers survive in solitary splendor in their own territories, bloated with the remains of former rivals that they have cannibalized. Heirs to a great fighting tradition, they have been domesticated by even larger corporate giants who employ them as both beasts of burden and of conflict — carriers of huge and profitable cargoes of advertising, and mercenaries to demonstrate the power of the system that sustains them. Newspapers may survive in this role for a long time, but it is difficult to imagine a return of their old vitality.

Newspapers have developed, increasingly, as carriers of advertising and other forms of service information. As they become less distinctive and essential to the public, they pave the way for new media that can perform their service functions more efficiently. Videotex, for instance, suffers from none of the confusion of purpose that paralyzes newspapers; it is able to provide every conceivable type of information or advertising to consumers on an individual basis.

Many newspaper readers still find it difficult to accept the notion that the newspaper stereotype that exists in their minds could be replaced by videotex as they imagine it. If and when the substitution occurs, it may not be as noticeable or as disruptive as expected. By then, newspapers may be providing little more in the way of news and comment than videotex can provide, and providing it in a massive tangle of advertising that videotex not only can simplify but make more serviceable in the form of teleshopping services on interactive videotex systems. The ability of these systems to provide information on demand to individuals breaks the link between news and advertising that has been characteristic of mass media in our society. Videotex users will consume information of various kinds according to their needs. News and editorial commentary will be one of many types of information; advertising will be another. No longer will it be necessary for both to come from the same source.

Newspapers have been attracted to videotex because it seems, at first, to be an electronic extension of their current publishing activities. They soon discover, in practice, that it is a medium that has relatively little to do with news, that news is only one of many services provided by videotex and probably not the most marketable.

For newspaper publishers, news is the product they sell to the consumer, and a large consumer market is what they sell to the advertiser. The symbiotic relationship between news and advertising no longer exists in videotex. In some of the early systems, news is seen as an incidental product of the system, or as a free premium for users who access a database containing primarily advertising and other commercial services.

It seems more and more doubtful that news, in the newspaper definition, will be the main economic engine or most valuable product of the industry. One recent estimate in the U.S. suggests that potential videotex users might be willing to spend about $5 per month for news services that they now receive "free" on radio and television. This is not a large pool of revenue to divide among many providers of specialized and therefore costly news services.

Publishers who have entered the new medium soon discover that their videotex activities bear less and less resemblance to their newspapers. This has occurred in Canada, where Infomart already thinks of itself as an "information utility" — a description that most newspapermen would find alien, if not threatening. Executives of Infomart have been taken from computer service companies, not from the ranks of the Toronto *Star* or Southam newspapers. Writers working for Infomart have come from advertising agencies, not from the newsrooms of newspapers. In the United Kingdom, where videotex experience is longer and more extensive, Rex Winsbury of Fintel, the electronic publishing subsidiary of the *Financial Times*, confessed, "We've almost totally forgotten our origins as a newspaper house."[1]

Newspapers in Germany, the Netherlands, and some other European countries still tend to see videotex as print publishing with a new means of delivery. Such British newspapers as the *Financial Times*, with more videotex experience, regard this as an experimental attitude that soon disappears within an operating system. In Prestel, Fintel has found itself competing not against other publishers, in the main, but against banks, mail order houses, travel agencies, and airlines, as well as new companies created specifically to serve videotex users. "It's quite a new landscape," according to Winsbury. "Our belief is that the applications of Viewdata (British videotex) are not to be seen purely in terms of promoting the traditional newspaper. If it's going to be a success, it's going to be a success in quite different ways from that."

As Torstar and Southam have demonstrated in Canada, large newspaper groups often have the capital and instincts to create videotex subsidiaries or divisions. In the early stages of videotex development, with many print publishers exploring the new medium, newspapers may feel more at home in videotex than do other industries. Infomart, for example, has perhaps found it easier to sell Telidon systems to publishing enterprises in the U.S. because of its relationship with the Toronto *Star* and Southam. This advantage may become less significant as videotex creates many new and distinctive "publishing" enterprises attuned directly to the needs of the new medium and its users. By then, the videotex activities of newspapers will be in a world of their own, far removed from the parent newspapers. Torstar's recent purchase of a mail-order house in the United States indicates the direction that videotex concerns may take as they exploit the advertising or "service information" aspect of videotex rather than news.

News and editorial comment stand apart from service information on videotex. They have distinctive functions. They require different policy approaches. Designers of the first videotex systems imagined that every newspaper with current news and archives stored in its computer would be in a position to publish on videotex. With distribution problems solved, newspapers would be launched electronically into a new world of competitive journalism.

Limited practical experience has demolished this utopian vision. It tends to show that one videotex system can serve a nation, as in Britain, and that one "electronic newspaper" or videotex news service of a general nature may be all that is needed, perhaps supplemented by a few specialized or regional news services. Because of its limited format, more suitable for reproducing headlines on the screen than for in-depth news analysis, videotex probably will tend to centralize the "processing" of news for the mass audience. It may be more inimical to competitive journalism than are the mass media today.

In Britain, where the Birmingham *Post* has established Viewtel and called it "the world's first electronic newspaper", no national rivals have appeared to compete with this initial venture. After little more than a year in operation, Viewtel is convinced that it has already established an effective monopoly on Prestel, partly because of the limited nature of the news it provides and the limited videotex news requirements of the ordinary Prestel user. It is difficult to imagine another national "electronic newspaper" offering anything except the same headlines and the same brief reports of international, national, and local events taken from the same news services.

This state of affairs seems to be taken for granted within Prestel, where it is regarded as being extremely unlikely that anybody could set up in serious competition with Viewtel. If competition did emerge, it probably would be from another established newspaper group rather than from a new source. Within Prestel, it is believed that Viewtel will "corner the market" even more effectively as times goes on because it charges users nothing for its news pages on Prestel, employing them to attract attention to its advertising pages.

Videotex trials in Canada now involve a small number of newspapers and newspaper groups. There is some danger that these pioneers may quickly establish an effective monopoly in the provision of a news service that could become one of our most important. If there is to be a single national "electronic newspaper", at least at the outset, it should be developed either by a public agency or by a newspaper cooperative.

Many people who appeared before the Commission to urge the creation of a state-owned newspaper or "print CBC" were not aware that the CBC was close to producing an "electronic newspaper" on teletext. Once the CBC teletext service is in operation, it will be a potential supplier of news on videotex.

Canadian Press already supplies a primitive form of teletext for cable TV systems which provide a print summary of news to their subscribers. Extending this service to make it an interactive videotex information system would be logical, efficient, and perhaps helpful to newspapers. Using CP might be one method of ensuring that part of the new revenues from videotex, earned by telephone or cable companies, could be used to sustain the journalistic base where news originates.

Some newspaper publishers predict that newspapers will become better in response to the challenge from videotex. If videotex supplies headlines and summaries of news, they say, newspapers of the future will become more like magazines, with more special features and editorial commentary. These forecasts do not confront the problem of producing this journalism of a higher order, by far the most expensive type, if advertising revenues of newspapers are threatened by videotex.

As videotex systems develop, the continuing viability of CP could be vital not only to newspapers but to the new medium. If videotex is going to be a market for the journalism produced by CP and its member newspapers, it is important that it does its share to maintain the quality of that journalism. Using either CP or a public agency as the primary "electronic newspaper" would reflect Canadian traditions and institutions.

Videotex systems in their entirety should also express a characteristic Canadian concern that communications systems be accessible to as many citizens as possible and that they serve national objectives. Even more than radio or television broadcasting, videotex will enable Canadians to communicate with one another, to share experience and knowledge with one another and, it is to be hoped, to understand one another better and to collaborate more closely in national endeavors. The creation of radio and television networks in Canada, and railroads in an earlier time, was inspired by a sense of national purpose. If videotex networks are to be the "railroads" of the information society, their financing and structure will be as important and probably as contentious for Canadian policymakers as were the railroads in the 19th century.

In its relationship with the federal government, Infomart has been perceived as the "Canadian Pacific" of Canada's emerging information society. It would be in the Canadian tradition now to explore the "Canadian National" parallel. Commercial development of electronic publishing may not ensure accessibility and the development of an adequate national service. Governments in Canada could study, as the Saskatchewan government has, the parallel or perhaps prior development of a state-run "electronic railroad" or, as it is more commonly called, "electronic highway", with connections or gateways to both public and private databases. Another version of the "Canadian National" approach might involve public databases, accessible to a wide variety of information providers, connected by "gateways" to existing carriers' networks.

News commentary and other types of personal journalism will benefit from the theoretical accessibility of videotex only if the new systems are structured to accommodate them. The role of government will be to ensure that videotex systems are as open as possible and that the "marketplace of ideas" that videotex would create is allowed to develop with a minimum of interference by government or corporate bureaucracies.

Canada is in a favored position to understand this new technology, to develop it, exploit it, and benefit from it. We have a solid foundation of theoretical studies in modern communications. Canada was one of the first countries to develop telegraph and telephone communications technology on a large scale and has consistently pioneered new applications. Technical progress has been accompanied by thoughtful attempts to develop appropriate communciations policy at federal and provincial levels. In communications, as in transportation in an earlier era, theoretical work and practical experience have helped us to define the public interest and to develop a system of state enterprise and private initiative to serve our best interests. The history of telegraph, telephone, radio, and television systems in Canada demonstrates this concern and achievement perhaps more clearly than does the record of any of our other national endeavors. This strong tradition has been evident, at times, in our first approaches to videotex and the emerging problems of the information society.

The decision to develop videotex in Canada was seen from the start, in the words of Jeanne Sauvé when she was minister of communications, as "an opportunity to introduce a system designed and manufactured by Canadians, and developed according to Canadian social and cultural needs". It may be our last opportunity, she said, "to innovate and refine a Canadian technology that will ensure a strong domestic electronics industry and contribute to the strengthening and enrichment of our cultural sovereignty".[2]

References

1. Interview, London, February, 1981.
2. Jeanne Sauvé, quoted in Science Council of Canada, *Communications and Computers*, Ottawa. 1978. p. 38.

15
Postscript: the new literacy

This study has dealt with an industry in transition, but the effect on newspapers of videotex development is a limited aspect of a world in transition.

The parallel and complementary development of computers and telecommunications in recent decades has been revolutionary, in the strictest sense of an overused word. It has affected every human activity, from the recording of the most intimate details of our lives to the management of state and corporate enterprises far beyond the capacity of earlier information technologies. And yet, as we have seen, we still seem to be on the threshold of this revolution. As individuals, we haven't fully grasped the implications of such a basic alteration in our methods of communicating with one another, nor have governments come to terms with changes that are creating a new definition of literacy and broadening society's traditional concern with education to include all forms of information.

As readers of the printed page, we still find it hard to associate reading with videotex. The act of reading is related, in our minds, with a liberating historical tradition of popular education and democratic government, as well as with personal rituals that delight us when we enter a bookstore or library, smell the atmosphere of printed pages, touch the volumes, and survey the customary arrangements of familiar typefaces. Reading newspapers gives us the same pleasurable sense of doing something that is habitual, entertaining, and useful.

The computer terminal has none of these graceful associations. We can't imagine curling up with one. The apparatus is associated with airline ticket counters, cash registers in department stores, and screens hidden behind the front desks of hotels and swivelling on the counters of stockbrokers. The screens are everywhere, and we accept them as useful, but we don't see anything uplifting or beautiful in them. The images that they display seem as crude to us as the first printed pages must have seemed, centuries ago, to those who used and loved the illuminated manuscripts which were the books of their own time.

Just as there are those who still practise calligraphy, and as the once-revolutionary craft of setting type for books by hand, printing them on durable paper, and binding them to last for centuries is still preserved among individual printers and bibliophiles, so there will always be the printed page. But, the screen already is alongside it in newspapers, schools, publishing houses, and libraries, the very temples of the old literacy. The lines that you now are reading had to appear on the screen of a word processor before they could be transferred to these pages.

The growth of these technologies has been swift and pervasive. They are here to stay. It is no longer a question of whether these systems will exist — but how they will develop.

The technology has outstripped our ability to comprehend it. As the screens multiply in our offices and start to invade our homes, academicians still are trapped in lengthy studies of man-computer communications, investigating whether we can work effectively, enjoyably, and even safely with computer terminals. The push of this technology is so strong, because of its usefulness, that we are adopting it with little understanding of what it will do to individuals and societies. The effects cannot help but be profound. When we alter the way in which we communicate with one another, we change everything to some extent. The proliferation of micro-computers in schools, for instance, is bound to affect teaching methods. The computers can encourage lazy teaching, or stimulate both teachers and students to work harder. Changes as elementary as this, in many areas of human activity, are too important to leave entirely to trial-and-error. They require a new commitment to the principles that have provided us in the past with the kind of education and access to information that is essential to our democratic society.

Although we have made attempts to do this in the past decade, the focus of development in practice has been narrow. Lip-service has been paid to the enormous changes required by the information society while the dollars have been spent primarily on the development of hardware and its commercial exploitation. In the search for immediate markets and employment, relatively little attention has been paid to the information content of the new systems and their impact on individuals and communities. The effects of videotex development on press concentration, on the quality of journalism, and on individual access to diverse sources of news, for instance, hardly has been considered in Canada in the headlong drive to promote Telidon as a competitor in the world videotex market.

This lack of direction often means, in fact, progress in the wrong direction. Without an underlying philosophy or idealism about new information technologies, we have tended to force new currents into old channels. Nothing illustrates this more graphically than the domination of our infant videotex industry by our largest information conglomerates.

We have endured the information revolution when we might have been expected to lead it. The problem does not lie in our technical competence. It has something to do with our difficulty in defining national objectives and acting together to achieve them. The revolution in information technology can aggravate or reduce this difficulty.

It seems inevitable that we will become one of the world's first information societies. This report on information technology and our newspapers ends with the realization that here is an opportunity to create among ourselves, taking advantage of our strengths, a uniquely literate and cultured example of the new society.

Appendices

APPENDIX I

Research contributors

1. Regulatory Aspects of the New Technology—Charles Dalfen

   A short history of regulation in newspapers, telephone, broadcasting, cable, and computer services. Possible regulatory approaches to the new technology.

2. Newspapers and Computers—Morrison W. Hewitt (Woods Gordon)

   History and current status of computerization in daily and weekly newspapers. Forecast of additional computer installations. Based on questionnaires.

3. New Technology and Ownership Concentration in Québec—Jean-Paul Lafrance in collaboration with Pierre Dumas and Guy Bertrand

   Study of the impact of new technology on the concentration of ownership and on francophone culture.

4. Newspapers and Videotex—Ian Brown and Robert Collison

   Corporate structure and future plans of Info Globe and Infomart, their status in the developing Canadian electronic information service industry. Collaboration between Infomart and the Department of Communications. Potential impact of videotex technology on newspapers.

5. Videotex Field Trials in Canada—Tom Paskal

   Checklist and progress report on 12 field trials as at April 1, 1981.

APPENDIX II

Selected bibliography

Barron, Iann, Ray Curnow, *et al*, *The Future with Microelectronics*. New York: Nichols Publishing, 1979.

Canada. Computer/Communications Task Force. *Report. Branching out*. Ottawa: Department of Communications, 1972. 2v.

Canada. Department of Communications. Telidon Information Kit. Ottawa: Information Services of the Dept., 1980.

Canada. Report of the Consultative Committee on the Implications of Telecommunications for Canadian Sovereignty (Chairman: J.V. Clyne). *Telecommunications and Canada*. Ottawa: 1979.

Canada. Telecommission. *Instant World: A Report on Telecommunications in Canada*. Ottawa: Dept. of Communications, 1971.

Chartrand, Robert Lee, and James W. Morenty, Jr., eds., *Information Technology Serving Society*. New York: Pergamon Press, 1979.

Christian, William, ed. *The Idea File of Harold Adams Innis*. University of Toronto Press, 1980.

Dertonyos, Michael L., and Joel Moses, eds., *The Computer Age: A Twenty-Year View*. MIT Press, 1979.

Evans, Christopher. *The Micro Millennium*. New York: Washington Square Press/Pocket Books, 1981.

Gardiner, W. Lambert (Scot). *Public acceptance of the New Information Technologies: The Role of Attitudes*. Gamma, Université de Montréal/McGill University, 1980.

Godfrey, David, *et al, Gutenberg Two*. Press Porcépic, 1980.

Innis, Harold Adams. *The Bias of Communication*. With an introduction by Marshall McLuhan. University of Toronto Press, 1979.

Inside Videotex. Proceedings of a seminar, March, 1980. Toronto: Infomart, 1980.

Madden, John C. *Videotex in Canada*. Ottawa: Department of Communications, 1979.

Martin, James, ed. *Future Developments in Telecommunications*. Prentice-Hall, 1977.

Martin, James. *The Wired Society*. Prentice-Hall, 1978.

Nora, Simon and Alain Minc. *The Computerization of Society: A Report to the President of France*. MIT Press, 1980.

Robinson, Glen O., ed. *Communications for Tomorrow: Policy Perspectives for the 1980s*. Toronto: Praeger Publishers, 1978.

Science Council of Canada. *Communications and Computers: Information and Canadian Society*. Ottawa: 1978.

Science Council of Canada. *A Scenario for the Implementation of Interactive Computer-Communications Systems in the Home.* Ottawa: 1979.

Serafini, Shirley and Michel Andrieu. *The Information Revolution and its Implications for Canada.* Ottawa: Department of Communications, 1980.

Sigel, Efrem, *et al. Videotex, The Coming Revolution in Home/ Office Information Retrieval.* White Plains, N.Y.: Knowledge Industry Publications, 1980.

Sindell, Peter S. *Public Policy and the Canadian Information Society.* Gamma, Université de Montréal/McGill University, 1979.

Smith, Anthony. *Goodbye Gutenberg.* Oxford University Press, 1980.

Thompson, Gordon B. *Memo from Mercury.* Institute for Research on Public Policy (occasional paper; no. 10). Montréal, 1979.

Tyler, Tim. *Electronics versus Paper Media.* San José, Calif.: SBS Publishing, May, 1979.

Valaskakis, Kimon. *The Information Society: The Issue and the Choices.* Gamma, Université de Montréal/McGill University, 1979.

Viewdata and Videotex, 1980-81. Transcript of Viewdata '80, first world conference on viewdata, videotex and teletext. White Plains, N.Y.: Knowledge Industry Publications, 1980.

Vista Directory and User Guide. Vol. no. 1, Teledirect. Toronto, Montréal: May, 1981.

Winsbury, Rex. *The Electronic Bookstall.* London: International Institute of Communications, 1979.

Winsbury, Rex. *New Technology and the Press*: A Study of the Experience in the United States for the Royal Commission on the Press. London: HMSO, 1975.

Woodrow, R. Brian *et al*, Conflict over Communications Policy: A Study of Federal Provincial Relations and Public Policy. Montréal: C.D. Howe Institute, 1980.

Woolfe, Roger. *Videotex*, London: Heyden & Sons, 1980.

Index

AT&T 38-9, 83-5
Alberta Press Case 86
Antiope 17,34,39
Apple Computer Inc. 58
Bell Canada
    Content control 88-9
    Fibre optics 57
    Vista 52-3,63-4,80
Blackburn, Walter J. 85-6
Bown, Herbert G. 45
Britain
    New technology 25-32
    Royal Commission on the Press 3
CBC 55-6,104
CNCP Telecommunications 57
Cable television
    Interactive 40,56-7
    On-screen print 40
    Rogers Cablesystems Inc. 40,56-7,64,91-2
    Telephone companies, competition 57
    Teletext 91-2
    Videotex 92
Canadian Labor Congress 86
Canadian Press, The 104-5
Canadian Radio-television and Telecommunications Commission 91
Carlisle, David 63,64,68,87
Carney, Pat 86
Ceefax 27
Channel 2000 40-1
Clyne Committee 23,99
Communications, Department of
    Infomart, relationship 87,98-9,105
Communications policy
    Federal-provincial jurisdiction 90
Compuserve 40, 41
Computers
    Home 40-1,57-8
    On-line 40-1
    Services, imports, exports 78
Duff, Sir Lyman 86
France
    "Electronic telephone directory" 33
    Newspapers, technological change 34-5
    Telecommunications 17,32-4
Fraser, J.W. 74
GTE 39
Gaffen, Fritz 64
Ganley, Oswald H. 78,90
Godfrey, David 86-7,89-90,96
Honderich, Beland 64

Info Globe 5-6,61,63,64
Infomart 54,55,58,61,63-4,87,96-9,103,105
Innis, Harold 21-2
Information society
    Forecasts 7-10
    Newspapers 10-2
Japan
    New technology 36-7
McLuhan, Marshall 21-2
Madden, John C. 48-9,97
Megarry, Roy 10
New technology
    Canada 22-3,104-5
    Public policy 22-3,105-6
    Terminology 15
    Theoretical studies 21-2
    Transborder data flows 77-80
    Union jurisdictions 56
    See also
    Computers
    Teletext
    Videotex
Newspapers
    Computers 2-6
        Electronic publishing
            Telegraph Journal/ Evening Times 55
            Toronto *Globe and Mail* 63
            Toronto *Star* 62
            Winnipeg *Tribune* 54
        Foreign ownership 79-80
        Technological revolution 1-6,107-8
        Toronto *Globe and Mail* 95
        Videotex
            Competition, relationship 34-5,57,85-7
            "Electronic newspaper" 104-5
            Invasion of privacy 73-5
            Journalists, copyright 71-3
            Viewtel 202 29-31,104
Omnitex 53
Oracle 27
Ostry, Bernard 74
Parkhill, Douglas 73,87,88,97
Prestel 16,26,27-32,68,74,88,104
    See also
        Viewtel 202
Project Grassroots 54, 63-4
Project Ida 53-4,63-4,75
Rogers Cablesystems Inc. 40,56-7,64,91-2
Satellite communications 80,95
Sauvé, Jeanne 23,24,47,105-6
Smith, Anthony 87
Southam Inc. 61-3
TV Ontario 55
Task Force on Privacy and Computers 77
Talbot, Robert 81
Télécable Vidéotron 81

Teledirect 96

Teleglobe Canada 56,79

Telephone companies
    Cable television, competition 57
    Carrier/content, videotex systems 87-9,92
    Optical fibre 57
    Videotex publishing 33-4,39,85-6

Teletel 33

Teletext
    Broadcast 90-1
    CBC 104
    Canadian Press 104
    Cable 91-2
    Description 16-7
    Field trials 55-6
    Various countries 16-7
        Britain 27,29
        France 33-4
        United States 39-40
        West Germany 35

Telidon
    Availability 48
    Background 45-6
    Cost 46-7
    Description 17,46
    Development 49
    Forecasts 67-9
    Foreign competition 48-9
    Importance 47,52
    Info Globe 63
    Infomart 64,97-8
    Information consortium 97
    Low-resolution 47
    Private industry 49
    Science Council of Canada, recommendations 98
    Teletext 55-6
    Transborder data flow 79
    U.S. market 48

Thomson Newspapers Limited 61,63

Thompson, Gordon 52,68-9

Torstar 62,63,64

United States
    New technology 37-42,58

Videotex
    Accessibility, national objectives 105,108
    Advertising 68,89
    Billing for services 73-4
    Broadcasting legislation 79
    Cable 92
    Carrier-content separation 31,39,53,87-9,92
    Carriers, regulatory decisions 83-6
    Competition 57
    Concentration of ownership 95-9
    Databases, Canadian ownership 79-80
    Definition, description 15-6,17
    Difficulties, deficiencies 18-9
    Field trials
        Bell Canada (Vista) 52-3,63-4,80
        Conclusions 51-2
        Federal government 55

    International 56
    Manitoba Telephone System 53-4, 64
    Various provinces 55
Freedom of the press 86
French-language databases 80-2
Future of 67-9
"Gateway" technique 29
Home computers, distinction 41-6
Impact, human behavior 19
Information providers 87
Libel 73
New literacy 107-8
News services 102-3
Privacy, invasion of 73-5
Québec, province of 80-1
"Telemetering" 74
Telephone 88-9, 92-3
Various countries 16-7, 35-6
    Britain 25-7, 27-31
    France 33-5
    Japan 36-7
    United States 37-42
    West Germany 35
See also
    New Technology
    Newspapers
    Various services

Viewtel 202 29-31, 104
Viewtron 17
Vista 52-3, 63-4, 80
Weekly press 4
West Germany
    New technology 35
Wilson, Larry 88-9
Winsbury, Rex 10, 103

Ministry of Education, Ontario
Information Centre, 13th Floor,
Mowat Block, Queen's Park,
Toronto, Ont.   M7A 1L2